W9-CDE-423

LIVING BY GOD'S SURPRISES

LIVING BY GOD'S SURPRISES

The glory of prayer in
suffering, mystery, weakness, and joy
A personal journey

HAROLD L.
MYRA

WORD BOOKS
PUBLISHER
WACO, TEXAS

A DIVISION OF
WORD, INCORPORATED

LIVING BY GOD'S SURPRISES

Library of Congress Cataloging-in-Publication Data

Myra, Harold Lawrence, 1939–
Living by God's surprises.

1. Prayer. 2. Myra, Harold Lawrence, 1939–
I. Title.
BV220.M97 1988 248.3′2 88–1293
ISBN 0–8499–0631–8

Printed in the United States of America

8 9 8 0 1 2 3 9 FG 9 8 7 6 5 4 3 2 1

“Great things happen to those who pray.”

CONTENTS

INTRODUCTION

Living by God's surprises. I find myself an unlikely person to write on this topic. Personally, I prefer an organized, tidy life. Unlike my wife, Jeanette, who is gloriously spontaneous, I like even my trips to the drugstore planned out. God can go ahead and surprise me all he wants, be as creative as possible, but I wish he'd make those surprises the sort that are immediately discernible as blessings. If there must be unpleasantness, I'd prefer it to be like the icy jolt of entering a swimming pool on a hot day; mere seconds later, the iciness is forgotten and the coolness welcomed.

Yet as I've read the more thoughtful Christians who write about their experiences in living by God's unexpected plans, it becomes clear that his surprises are not always immediate blessings. The life of faith is not like opening Christmas gifts every day. God's surprises disrupt; they humble; they amaze; they delight; and they come mixed up in messy ways with irritations and anguish.

Despite my dislike for disruptions, I've become intrigued by God's persistence in working this way. Moreover, it's become clear that if there is any way at all in which we can participate and see it happening, it will be through his chosen way of working—through prayer.

Some years ago I was sitting at breakfast in a JoJo's

restaurant with Ernie Owen, longtime friend and publisher. I shared with him some of the things that had been happening recently within our church prayer group where I had seen God working remarkably in people who were living through the worst of circumstances: the death of children, sexual abuse, attempted murder, divorce, and fatal accidents. In each instance prayer was the vital linkage to their hope and growth.

"Even so," I told Ernie, "though I've prayed most of my life, about a year ago I came to a conclusion. I realized that deep, deep down I didn't believe in prayer." As I said them, the words seemed strange and foreign on my tongue.

"My actions were what convinced me. If prayer were the very center of my life, if I believed all the Bible says about it, I'd obviously pray more. At the same time, however, I began to see prayer as the essential gate through which God takes action in our lives, and it began to make a difference in the way I approached prayer—and in the way I prayed."

For several years after that breakfast Ernie kept encouraging me to write about what I was experiencing and learning about the way God works through prayer in our lives. "Just tell the story," he said.

We were both interested not only in "marvelous answers" to prayer, but in the discouraging, confusing answers. And what about the times our prayers seem to go maddeningly unanswered? Or when, despite our prayers, fellow Christians betray us or create tragic misunderstandings? Or when brutality strikes the innocent beside us? Or when we simply cannot pray as we wish?

Eventually I was able to set aside a month to begin exploring all this . The month was November, and I arranged to stay at my parents' home in the Pocono Mountains of Pennsylvania while they took a trip to Florida.

The usual setting for God's surprises is the ordinary,

everyday world. I found that thirty days in the forest accentuated both the glory and the simplicity of that world. The mountains and valleys, the Appalachian Trail, the deer and sunsets and waterfalls—all made by the Creator of surprises—blended with my ideas about prayer and God's invasions, teasing my thoughts, scooting them off in all directions.

We all live amid the ordinary, day after day. Yet in prayer we can ruminate on the extravagant, bewildering, magnificent way God invades our ordinary lives. Sometimes we don't really want that; often it's not at all comfortable. But in a sense, we have no choice. He will be at work in us, one way or the other. Through prayer, however, we can become aware and sensitive participants in the drama.

As Henri Nouwen has said, "You begin to suspect that to pray is to live."

Here, then, are my reflections on my November in Pennsylvania.

1
LIVING BY PARADOX

It is early November, but a light snow is already falling. I watch through the windows as it lands on the huge evergreens and maples snugged up against my parents' house. I recall planting some of those trees when they were knee-high. Now their branches tower above this simple but spacious two-story home my father built, evenings and weekends, while I was still in school.

This entire month I'll spend alone here in the Pocono Mountains of eastern Pennsylvania. Back in Chicago, my wife and children bade me godspeed as I set off to be a hermit here, to hike and write and pray. My parents, full of love and warm wishes, have driven off to Florida with their modest travel trailer. I am alone with my books and writing pads and notes.

It seems appropriate to start writing about prayer in this house, for it was here as a young boy that I prayed earnestly every night, for God to bring me close to him, and it was here as a high school senior that he entered my life with great force. Here, when I was fifteen, I prayed brashly about the first day of deer season; and whatever one may think of mystic coincidences, the events that day made it seem God spoke aloud into the cold December air. Here, as a teenager, I knelt at the church rail each New Year's Eve in fervent prayer and rose after midnight full of fresh hope and resolve for the new year.

Yet I also began to learn of God's silences in this place.

The setting is idyllic. A ten-minute hike takes you to the Appalachian Trail which cuts along the top of Kittatinny Mountain, rising like some friendly giant in front of our house. When I was young, my mother would sit on the lawn looking at that mountain and say, "Harold, I don't know why we have it so good." I would always agree with her, which is one reason none of us was enthused twenty years ago when the federal government bought their land and hundreds of other homes and farms to create the Delaware Water Gap National Recreation Area. My parents opted for life rights; as far as I know, they are the only ones besides the rangers living inside the park.

The snow settling on the green boughs outside evokes memories of cutting Christmas trees and branches in these very woods. We would shake off the snow and drag them home, bringing that biting smell of sap into the house.

This is my favorite place in all the world, where love and God's peace and grateful nostalgia blend with the deer on the front yard searching for apples, the rabbits scooting across the snow-whitened grass, and the squirrels running off the tops of trees in suicide missions that are actually show-off acrobatics. Around the room are photos of my family: my wife Jeanette and our children Michelle, Todd, and Greg smile happily from photos. On the wall above the red sofa hangs the large, familiar painting of the resurrected Jesus walking with his two disciples on the road to Emmaus.

Idyllic. Just like the nature photographs on church bulletins and devotional books, or the cozy photos from a family album.

Yet there are other photos and other realities, other memories. Close by the bright montage of my children are framed snapshots of my cousins, Lois and David. They were my only cousins, in some ways more like siblings, part of our intimate family circle. Lois, a pretty blonde in her late teens, is wearing a big yellow sunhat, sitting by the Pinebrook Bible Conference pool. She was with me at that pool the day I met Ted Engstrom twenty-five years ago and got my first coveted job in journalism. But only a few years later her brother David was to call me in Chicago and tell me, "Your darling cousin is dead." I will never forget those words crashing into me. Lois, who had just received her commission as a nurse in the Air Force, had been killed when her car skidded off the road and into a culvert. The image of the basement room where I answered that call and my stunned reaction are still frozen in my memory.

The school photo of David shows a serious, athletic-looking young man who was headed for medical school and the mission field. At Lois's funeral he spoke about a corn of wheat falling into the ground and dying.

David was to confront those same thoughts again a decade later. Across this room in which I write another photo shows an older Dave with his young children. His wife Elsbeth, a Swiss missionary nurse he had met in Nigeria, is missing from the picture. She had just died of leukemia, and the look on David's and the children's faces brings back all those eighteen months of her dying and her wrestling with God.

Photos of my brother Johnny and me are like shots of a dozen different boys, so changed at various ages: from long blond curls to schoolboys posing with Angora rabbits and goats and puppies, then both of us in Marine Corps uniforms. Newer color photos show Johnny's first two sons and daughter at various ages, but their mother's photo is not here. After seventeen years of marriage, divorce brought hostility, pain, outrage, the wounding of young and old. Since then Johnny has remarried and his youngest son beams out happily from another frame.

If I walk through the dining area to a west window, I can see through the falling snow a small, one-story white house at the far edge of the lawn. Beside it is a small house trailer collapsed in on itself. I remember the day when a huge truck turned into Granddad's driveway carrying the entire pre-cut house in thousands of boards, studs, and shingles jutting from both sides, making the vehicle as wide as our little dirt road. The drivers dumped everything next to that small trailer, where my grandparents lived. For years afterward, Granddad was building the house. He was an unhappy person, my mother's father, his life strewn with failure. But he had chosen a wonderful wife. Everyone loved Grandmom; we all thought her a saint. Then she died, and Granddad's paranoia increased the tensions between him and my family. Finally he completed a few rooms and moved into the house.

One winter day when I was in my late teens I went over to visit him and found him dead on the cold linoleum between the kitchen and the living room. I walked home and told my mother, "Granddad's dead."

"Are you sure?"

"Yes, I'm sure. He's dead." And unspoken between

us was a curious mixture of sadness, relief, and perplexity. Granddad had been a Christian man; I had heard him pray. Yet he came to the end of life frustrated and bitter.

No, the setting might be idyllic, but not our family. We were, and are, thoroughly human.

The lamp base on the table by my hand was once a bowling pin. Turned on a lathe to strip it down to the natural wood, grooved like thick rope, then stained and lacquered, it was made for my mother by Richie when he was around twelve. My parents took Richie and his retarded brother, Royal, in as foster children when Richie was five and Royal two. Seven years later, against my parents' wishes, the state returned the two boys and their sisters to their mother.

Richie eventually got into drugs, ran away from home, and hid in my granddad's deserted trailer, which then still had a roof on it. No one realized Richie was there until recently widowed Mrs. Prosser, my parents' nearest neighbor, noticed him prowling around and told the police. She told my mother she was scared. Then Richie appeared in her driveway one day, and she threatened to call the police. In a blurred panic he shot her in the face with a shotgun, and she lay there in the driveway and bled to death.

Today Richie is serving a life sentence in the state prison in Dallas, Pennsylvania; he has been there for fifteen years. Yesterday he called me, and it reminded me of the day I took my family to visit him. As we drove up the long hill approaching the prison, moving closer and closer to the barbed wire and rambling brick buildings, I asked Jeanette and our three children, "How must it have felt riding up this hill in handcuffs at seventeen years of age, knowing you would spend the rest of your life here?"

My daughter Michelle is now seventeen. She's beautiful, bright, a gymnast and honors student, a believer.

What a different future ahead of her than the one Richie faced at her age.

Outside, the snow falls straight and hard against the green trees, like sheets of sparkling stars. Inside, the room's store of memories haunts me in a strange mixture of shocks and joys, of self-inflicted wounds and gentle triumphs, of weakness and God's grace. On the wall beside the west window is a Viking ship along with bright red and blue Norwegian flags and other mementos of trips to Oslo, Stavanger, Kristiansand, and Skien, where my father grew up.

The photo of my Norwegian cousin Hjordis, her husband, Johan, and their two daughters lifts my spirits. A decade ago Hjordis and her mother came from Stavanger for their first visit. Industrious, vivacious, attractive, Hjordis was also thoroughly suspicious of religion. "You may not like being with these people," her mother had told her before they came. "They pray before meals." But over the course of several years and three lengthy visits with us and many of our relatives, the whole family found a living faith. One summer Jeanette and I and the kids stayed for ten days with them at their home in Stavanger. Hjordis and Johan have added a special dimension to the spiritual life of their Lutheran church; their faith is contagious. One of their daughters is attending Bible school. It would seem that our prayers for Hjordis and her family played at least some part in this work of grace, and they, too, are now people of prayer.

Grace. God's grace in our all-too-human lives. Even Richie is a story of grace. He entered prison barely able to write a letter; now he is articulate with words and proficient with his typewriter. From all indications he is deeply committed to Christ. But why did his story have to include Mrs. Prosser's violent death? Why didn't our early prayers for him prevent his agonies?

Recently I talked with an older pastor and his wife about the bitter tragedies in their children's lives. Deep sorrow has aged their faces; it has also etched lines of grace and insight. After talking to them, I wrote this on a card:

Expect the worst;
Expect the best;
The best is yet to come.

As I sit here watching the falling snow, I think of Jesus' words, "In this world you shall have troubles." Yet he also said that he had overcome the world. Too often in our lives tragedy waits just over the next hill. But when it comes, we also find God at work in surprising ways.

~

Evening again. The snow has melted during the day. I step into the front yard, heading for the lake, but the sunset stops me. It lights up the whole sky. I can't resist turning a slow 360 degrees, shaking my head in wonder.

To the east and north, white clouds at the horizon turn gray, then lavender and purple. South, above Kittatinny Mountain, a great flock of blue and gray clouds chase a few pink strays—iridescent puffs escaping across the blue sky. In the west, a giant black smudge is edged with a brilliant band of sunset red, with wisps of white floating above it like bits of curly hair lifting off a flat red skull. All this extends above and around me, spread like a sky-wide Indian blanket.

But in five minutes the whole thing is gone, except for one red column drifting toward me from the sun.

Slides and home movies of sunsets bore us. What ingratitude! How can we not be awed by such celestial phantasmagoria? Strange, though. When I lived here, I seldom noticed sunsets. How could I have missed all those opportunities for gratitude and praise?

It takes a mere three minutes to walk to Prosser's Lake, which is actually a one-acre pond. In the late forties, shortly after my family moved here from the city, Johnny and I watched the bulldozers dig this lake out of the swamp. I stand now on Mr. Prosser's forty-year-old dock, still solid and uncracked. Reflecting up at me are birches, Scotch pines, spruces, a huge willow framed against the mountain. Sunfish poke their noses into the captured images of clouds. A few yards out on the bottom I spot the outline of an old rowboat, all that is left of the original that had once been bright orange. It brings back a wash of memories of David and Lois and me diving off it after supper, laughing, shouting, splashing till the moon was high.

Across the road from the lake, spruces sixty feet high stand half naked, one side of their branches burned off right to the top. A decade ago two boys came to my parents in the night exclaiming, "The house is on fire!" By the time Mother and Dad got there, Prosser's house was a conflagration. My parents wondered if the boys had been playing with matches. They denied it, but later we learned they had indeed caused the fire.

Beside the burned spruces, water leaps from a black pipe. I remember the day the giant drilling truck turned from the little dirt road onto the lawn and past the old well—a Disney-like wishing well of fieldstones, complete with crank, bucket, rope, and peaked roof. There's no trace of it now. Mr. Prosser had built it on his weekend escapes from his Wall Street brokerage firm; he worked like a peasant here on the flowers, lawn, trees, and barn, dressed like a tramp, much to the amusement of my mother. An accomplished portraitist, he painted an owl on the front of his big old barn and on the side two boys on skis schussing down a mountain. The figures were a good twenty feet high; he said they were Johnny and me. A few years ago they pulled down the barn, and I miss those fading skiers.

A little further down the road is a clearing in the woods. This is where Mrs. Prosser died. As a widow, she had built a second house, modern, beautifully landscaped. It was torn down after her death. Now only the clearing is left.

In the deepening dusk I top a rise in the road and see through the trees the same sunset, but totally new. It's a thick strip of rich salmon now, with a dark cloud above it like a fat lid. The black trees stand out against the orange, mysterious and worlds away.

Just beyond those trees I can smell another barn that burned down just a few days ago, torched by arsonists. It was at least a hundred years old with hand-hewn timbers. The miscreants also tried to set fire to a house nearby in which a family slept—two parents and small children. The only reason the house didn't burn was that the arsonists had ignited kitty litter that turned out to be the nonflammable kind. The young family was awakened by firemen long after the barn, two big trucks, and a car were destroyed. If the kitty litter had ignited, they probably would have died.

Idyllic, these mountains. The beauty of sunsets and trees can catch at your throat. Neighbors wave at you as you drive past. But here also are people who will burn beautiful old barns and little children.

"Call unto me, and I will answer thee, and show thee great and mighty things, which thou knowest not." I vividly recall that announcement from God in Jeremiah 33:3 as a magnificent challenge flung at me in college, a challenge and a promise. It filled me with such hope that my mother still talks about hearing me long before I reached the driveway in my battered '49 Plymouth, singing hymns at the top of my lungs. During college, I worked with high school Bible clubs, and although I didn't like the games and chitchat and would have preferred to stay at home and read, out of duty came joy, as Mother Teresa puts it.

"Call unto me, and I will answer. . . ." The verse still resonated in me after college when I packed my little Datsun for Chicago. By the time ten years had passed, I was thinking: If while I was growing up I had developed an ultimate fantasy plan for my life—trips to the moon, anything at all—I could not have conjured up as meaningful a life as God is giving me. Had not my prayers been answered far, far beyond my expectations? Not that I had become rich or famous. But I was doing work I relished, with people I respected, and I had married the woman I loved.

"Great and mighty things"? Yes they were. Over the past twenty-five years it would seem that God has kept his bargain. All my "calls" have been answered in "great and mighty ways"—but strictly on God's terms. Sometimes illogically; sometimes distressingly. This call to adventure has been a strange mixture of tedium, trauma, accomplishment, anger, frustration, amazement, ecstasy, and bewilderment. Ironically, he doesn't seem as concerned as I about getting out his own gospel; he has allowed some of his best servants to be stricken with cancer, others to be torn by circumstances or bizarrely self-destructing. Fervent prayer sometimes seems to change nothing at all. God is not, as C. S. Lewis indicates, a tame lion, nor does he answer prayers like a full-service agency.

I remember a dozen years ago walking to Prosser's Lake with David and Elsbeth. Two days later, back in Chicago, Jeanette and I received a call from David saying that Elsbeth had acute leukemia. Over the next eighteen months she called out to God from the depths of her soul, in anguish over leaving her husband and her little children. She had served God in Africa among the most primitive people, bringing them the gospel and medical care. Now her own prayers seemed to go unanswered.

And what can one say of Lois? That her father, a pastor utterly numbed by her death, had not prayed enough? Or of Granddad, dying alone and bitter? Or of Richie, for whom we have prayed for so long?

How many pious, godly souls have been struck down through the centuries, even as they prayed for deliverance? Yet despite all this—despite the impossible questions, the drab and tawdry times, the failures—we are still called upon to pray with, of all things, Great Expectations!

An absurdity. A paradox. Yet the gospel truth.

God, it seems, chooses to work in enigma and pain, with miracles as rare but as real as meteor flashes across a dark night.

2
LIVING BY COINCIDENCE

I am walking deep in the woods, curious about the white-tailed deer I might flush out. Leaves and dead branches crunch underfoot. Could Indians on moccasins go silently over a bed of crisp oak leaves? I envision myself floating silently over the ground, propelled by a hand rocket in each fist, the way stunt men fly around with them as if they were in space. I'd love to float up over the deer and stare down at them.

The deer are a tease. At the slightest sound they leap loudly into flight, their graceful bodies barely visible but their white tails bobbing up and down in the tree-blurred distance—like animated fantasy creatures, bobbing in the forest just beyond reach.

The trail I am following has enchanted me since childhood. It leads to acres of massive pines beside a rushing creek. The lowest branches are high overhead, blocking the sun. Brown needles form a thick, luxurious carpet from the foot of the mountain down the embankment to the creek itself. Bright green laurel surround the naked hardwoods.

Deer sign is everywhere: pressed grass where they slept, scuffed leaves, droppings. As I follow the sign, sure enough, I hear one bounding off and see its tail in the distance. I follow its trail and eventually find areas where the deer have scraped away needles and black dirt to expose tree roots.

The deer has led me further along this trail than I've gone before. It is petering out to a barely discernible path through the laurel. I have to bull my way through. Suddenly I break out into a boulevard someone has widened and cut.

After a few minutes on this wide trail, the totally unexpected happens. Instead of white tails and shadowy forms dancing in the distance, a big doe crashes out of the thick laurel and bounds right onto the trail beside me! She's as startled as I. She stands not ten feet away, motionless, staring at me with curiosity. Finally, after at least a full minute, she sedately walks off.

Now you see 'em, now you don't. The deer are in the forest, but often all you get are glimpses. Like God's surprises.

Sometimes I walk the woods intently, examining each tree and bush closely, and catch sight of a deer furtively moving away. They probably do this all the time, even when I'm not watching for them. Surprises that never become surprises to me at all. But they're there all the time, like God at work in the world.

It's not often a deer jumps right onto the trail with you. But sometimes they do—as startlingly real as one of those highly specific answers to prayer that come along now and then.

The first time I had an experience of that sort involved, oddly enough, a five-point buck. For teenage boys growing up in the mountains of eastern Pennsylvania, getting one's first buck was a rite of passage. When I was a high school sophomore, the night before the first day of buck season, I had probably never prayed more selfishly nor more specifically. "Lord," I said, "I'd rather not even see a buck than shoot and miss, or wound him. You place the shot. I ask not only that you bring the buck, but that you put the bullet exactly where you want it."

The next morning, my brother Johnny got his buck early. By 4:30 I still hadn't seen any deer. In half an hour, shooting would be over for the day. Yet I had an odd sense of total peace that I would get my buck.

At 4:50 I heard a shot far down the mountain. I was sitting under a cedar, staring into the darkening woods, thinking, "That guy got his just ten minutes before closing." Suddenly I heard a deer running up the mountain toward me. It was a buck. It stopped about fifty yards away and seemed to stare right at me. Carefully I took aim at its head with my Winchester 30-30 and slowly pulled the trigger. I was startled at the way the animal instantly collapsed. Down the hill I raced, exultant. It was a beautiful five-point buck! I found a wound on its foreleg—the shot from down the mountain—but no sign of where my bullet had hit him. No wound in the head, neck, or chest.

It wasn't until I had the deer hanging up at home that I saw what had happened. The bullet had entered its eye without so much as touching the bones around it. I was amazed by this, especially in light of my repeated prayers that God would place the bullet. Perfect placement. Absolutely dead center!

One may rightfully ask whether or not God works like this. Is he in the business of answering such relatively trifling, adolescent requests while ignoring life-and-death prayers from people like Elsbeth? Yet the placement of that bullet seemed as real an answer to a boy groping for faith as a deer leaping onto the trail with me today. Perhaps it was coincidence; perhaps it was God nudging me toward faith.

The experience reminds me of a story often told by the late V. Raymond Edman, who was president of Wheaton College. He had been a young soldier during World War I, slogging through raw, wet conditions, praying for a place to sleep. Through a series of events that would also seem like coincidences, he ended up in "a feather bed for Christmas." The event contributed to Edman's fondness for saying, "Never doubt in the dark what God has told you in the light."

Perhaps it seems immature to take seriously such "answers" to prayers for hunting, or for a place to sleep, or for lost pins. Yet Jesus calls us to a childlike faith. Such coincidences are never frequent enough, never conclusive enough to give proof of God at work. They are occasional flashes rather than a steady stream we can come to expect, rely on, or manipulate. Yet those who pray fervently encounter enough of them to build a certainty that "something's going on."

God connects with us in prayer in patterns as diverse as his creation. Prayer is enigmatic, but as real as electricity. Oswald Chambers asserts that prayer is "God's chosen way of working," and indeed one can look at the entire Bible as a sort of dialogue, a continuous prayer exchange. Throughout Scripture we find prayers in many forms. Daniel prayed three times a day, and his faith was immovable in a hostile, foreign land. David asked God to "teach his fingers to war." Job voiced his sorrow and complaints. Jesus spent all night in prayer.

~

I sit at the kitchen table and use a Norwegian cheese slicer to cut four wafer-thin pieces of light brown Gjetost onto a slice of bread and pour a cup of tea. In this same room about five years after the incident with the buck, I prayed about my plans to attend a two-week Youth for Christ school in Kansas City. For some reason the thirty-two hour bus ride seemed important, so I prayed earnestly and specifically that God would make the trip a powerful introduction to my youth ministry, that he would take control of all those thirty-two hours. What happened on that bus went far beyond my expectations.

As I got on the Greyhound, I recognized a pretty, dark-haired girl I had known in high school and sat down beside her. I had prayed for her many times, and we had nearly dated, but she ultimately thought me "too religious." During the hour ride to Easton, our first stop and her destination, we had a pleasant conversation. Her presence at the very start of the journey seemed an omen, and I prayed for her as I watched her walk down the city street toward her college.

More passengers got on at this stop, among them two young women and an Air Force sergeant. He looked Italian, handsome and dark with a neatly trimmed mustache. The younger of the two women, an attractive, petite redhead, was about nineteen. She carried a baby in her arms. Her seatmate was in her late twenties, a striking Mexican woman dressed in a ruffled white skirt and blouse.

Our bus entered the Pennsylvania Turnpike and we rode for hours up and down the long mountains and through the dark tunnels under them. The two women and the sergeant chatted with great animation, like old friends. At times I caught snatches of their conversation. I knew they had just met, yet some mysterious common experience was bonding them together.

A few hours from Pittsburgh, I moved to a seat beside

the sergeant. We talked for awhile, and it soon became clear what the three had in common. The man had just come home from service in Korea. He told me how all through his years overseas he had longed to be with his wife and had eagerly waited for their reunion. But when he arrived in the States, she had rejected his embraces. He was stunned to learn she was determined to marry another man.

Then he nodded toward the young girl with the red hair sitting across the aisle from us, as quiet and subdued as the baby in her arms. She was leaving her husband, he told me, going back to her parents in Iowa. He didn't say anything about the other woman, but I learned shortly afterward that she, too, was leaving her husband.

It had begun snowing hard by the time we stopped in Pittsburgh. I got out to stretch after the long ride, and when I came back from the terminal I found they had switched us to another bus. As we headed across Ohio against the deepening snow, the lunch I had left in my seat was heading in another direction.

The snow delayed us, piling up deeper and deeper, and we skipped a scheduled meal stop to make up time. I thought longingly of my lost sandwiches. I again sat next to the Air Force sergeant, listening to his story, but also having a chance to talk and share my faith. The passengers seemed to be growing edgy, yet that strong camaraderie emerged, such as is often evident when strangers face a common difficulty.

Someone started singing. Christmas was long past, but the white flakes covering the rolling Ohio hills evoked Christmas carols, and soon the whole bus joined in as the driver kept trying to make up time through the snow.

At midnight, we were moving slowly through a little town. The Mexican woman was sitting beside me now, next to the window, and we could see an occasional pedestrian walking against the gusts of snow or stepping into a small coffee shop with steamy windows.

"This must be a difficult trip for you," I said to her.

"My husband kicked me out," she replied softly. Her Spanish accent made it a bit difficult for me to understand, and I had to listen carefully.

"What do you mean? What happened?"

"He just kicked me out. We had been married only six weeks. Now I have to go back to Mexico."

"How can that be?" I asked, looking over at her beautiful face and starting to feel angry at her husband. "What happened?"

Instead of explaining the details, she simply said, "I am his fourth wife. He has done this three times before."

The big wipers stroked away the blinding flakes that were hitting the windshield; thin bits of snow drifted past our side window. But the cozy small-town scene that looked like a Norman Rockwell print had suddenly become cold and harsh. I felt the coldness of my own silence; yet I had no response. What her husband had done seemed so monstrous.

The bus moved on out of the town, and by the time the lights of the next village appeared, the Mexican woman and I were talking about God and Jesus and hope. I told about how much Jesus loved her; how all she had to do was reach out to him in prayer. We both prayed for the forgiveness of sins. She prayed that God would fully enter her life, and I prayed with her that God would give her a new future. As we rode on, she finally fell asleep, and I kept praying for her in the darkness.

In the morning, very early, we stopped in a small town in Iowa. The red-haired young woman wrapped her baby securely in its blankets and stepped out into the swirling snow. A middle-aged couple standing in the windy street quickly stepped forward. I assumed they were her parents, though they seemed awkward as they embraced her and the baby she held. Tears welled as I watched the four of them walk away against the winter wind. The young woman looked like many of the kids I worked with in Bible clubs, the kids who were my reason for traveling to the training school in Kansas.

At the next stop, the Mexican woman had to change buses. We talked now like old friends, and as we parted I handed her some Christian literature and my address.

"Write to me," I said. "I'll be praying for you, and I want to help any way that I can." I stood in the terminal and waved goodby to my new friend as her Greyhound noisily backed up. She waved back to me from her window, smiling a brave, sad smile. Again my eyes filled with tears.

During the few hours left on the trip, one thought kept recurring: How could God have possibly answered my prayers more specifically? He had allowed me to become part of a drama that fleshed out the training I was to begin. The opportunities to reach out to these three people had been natural and compelling. Was it really because I had prayed so much about this trip?

Another thought also intrigued me as the Greyhound neared Kansas City. Had God prompted me to pray for the bus ride in the first place?

In contrast, the next two weeks were a rush of activity. I prayed little if any about my return trip. And the long journey home was thoroughly uneventful.

Coincidences connected by prayer. A handful of personal scenes stand out like high, white mountains, unusual in their clarity against the sky.

A dozen years after that bus ride to Kansas City I was sitting in an office in Wheaton, Illinois, wrestling with a major problem. Our organization sorely needed to sort out some major administrative problems, and I wondered if I should volunteer. I didn't want to; it would be straight administration, not magazine work.

But the need was critical, so I had been wrestling in prayer for days. Should I offer myself? My colleagues cautioned me against it, yet they had no alternatives. I figured my potential for failure in the position at a good fifty percent, yet leaving the vacuum was worse.

I kept praying, "Lord, stop me if this isn't your will. I can't look into the future and know if this is right or not. Close the door or open it. You've got to get involved; my brain just can't sort this out."

I studied the first chapters of Daniel and thought about how he had prayed three times a day and made his choices based on his communication with God. I read of Nebuchadnezzar eating grass out in the field like an animal because he wouldn't give the glory to God or follow him. In Daniel I saw what I wanted; in Nebuchadnezzar I saw what I was too frequently sucked into—the feeling that I could move from success to success, God tailing along somehow instead of being the central power and direction.

I paced my office and stared at the red brick wall. "Lord," I said, "the stakes are high. The lives of so many people will be affected. You have to take control of this." With those words on my lips, and a deep sense of God's peace within, I started down the hall to the president's office to offer my services. However, before I got to his door, he met me in the hall with a man he said was under consideration for the position.

The man and I talked in my office for forty-five minutes. He was an ideal candidate. And the timing of my meeting him at the president's door, having put it all into God's hands in fervent prayer, seemed to me a special sign.

Other cities and events come to mind which seemed at the time—and still seem so today—to be God responding to my prayers. All this is in keeping with Archbishop William Temple's idea that it's rather amazing how often the coincidences seem to stop when we stop praying. Exactly! Times of prayerlessness in my life never seem to produce these coincidences; they only come after intense prayer.

Of course, anything can be explained away. The five-point buck. The bus ride. Anything. As Frederick Buechner says, we see God's work clearly only "now and then." It's probably a good thing he doesn't constantly produce these coincidences or we'd be chasing them all the time. In fact, maybe we should put up signs on all these remarkable stories of answered prayer that appear in magazines and biographies: "Warning: Unusual Peak Experiences. Not to be expected weekly!" They're like mountain peaks from which we can view the rest of God's more subtle work.

I finish my lunch of Norwegian cheese, pop an Andes mint in my mouth for dessert, and begin cleaning up. Living alone has its advantages: I brush the crumbs off the plate, rinse out the cup, and I'm ready for my next meal. I can put off serious dishwashing for as much as a week.

As I put items back in the refrigerator, I'm thinking of a recent meeting of our prayer group in Illinois. As usual, about twenty of us had gathered in a small room in the church after the morning service. In previous weeks Don had asked us to pray for his son Luke who was to have open-heart surgery for the third time. Over the ten or so years in which Luke had struggled with congenital heart problems, we had often prayed for him, and he had come through his many traumas successfully. Now, Don reported, Luke had come through his latest surgery, and he went on to describe some rich spiritual experiences in the hospital.

We had also prayed the week before that Matt, our associate pastor, would find a buyer for his house. "Praise the Lord," he told us joyfully, "it sold."

Grace thanked the Lord for the birth of a granddaughter and for the baptism of her own daughter. We praised God for many such blessings, and we prayed for a woman who had just suffered a second miscarriage.

A lively discussion then ensued about how we are to view God's involvement in our lives. Several cautioned that we perhaps too quickly attribute events to God. Grace's husband, Jay, had been listening carefully. With Grace, he was equally thankful for the birth of their granddaughter and the baptism of their daughter. But he and Grace had sustained more than one tragedy over the years. A short time ago they had watched their son Ivan, a young man with a wife and small daughter, slowly die of cancer. As we sat there, Jay said intensely, "I'm glad, Matt, for your house being sold. Don, I'm glad for Luke's heart being okay. But I have a hard time saying God did it. Your son is alive; my son is dead." Jay paused, then added with simple eloquence, "I want him back." He quietly repeated it, his head bowed, his love for Ivan etched clearly in every word: "I want him back."

Jay is a brilliant man who knows firsthand the ambiguities of life. He has felt the terrible hooks of barbarous reality and knows even fervent prayer cannot always prevent them. A few weeks later I heard him praying for a sick child, and I recalled how he and Grace and many others had prayed fervently and constantly for their son while he was still alive. But Ivan died.

Coincidences. We can be glib about them. We can come to expect them, and when they don't appear, weave elaborate explanations for why our prayer "didn't work." We can forget that miracles—true miracles—are by their very nature infrequent. We can be presumptuous, even insensitive, to those who have faced the worst, while God seemed to do nothing no matter how hard they prayed.

Despite all that, Archbishop Temple's comment about coincidences and prayer contains an enigmatic truth. The tough questions all these complexities raise push us into more dialogue with God.

I glance up from my writing. Five o'clock. Almost dark. I look out the front door. A deer, barely discernible, is walking past our old well. Before we got running water inside, we sometimes had to prime that well with the juice from a can of peas.

I slip on my shoes and jacket, then try to open the back door silently. As I step onto the back porch, I see a dark shape on the lawn. It's a big doe, staring at me under the light. I freeze. We gaze at each other. She moves her ears, listening, peering.

I step onto the gravel driveway and notice another deer in the road. The doe bounds off toward him, rustling the leaves. The light is strange in this nether time between light and darkness, with artificial light from the porch filtering through the dusk.

I look toward the lake. The road is a narrow tunnel to the red light of the sunset shining through the great masses of dark trees. The glow at the end of the tunnel rises into the dark sky and is swallowed up. Black clouds are illumined below in pastels, like globs floating east, away from the colors that spawned them.

The deer are gone. The wonders of sunset and dusk turn into night.

Now I see nothing but the lights from the house.

3
LIVING BY SURPRISE

Mid-afternoon I walk beyond the lake, past the clearing where Mrs. Prosser died, to the bend of the road just before the rise by the barn that burned last week. Red berries brighten the woods on both sides of the road, hundreds of them in thick clumps like miniature grape clusters. Did I ever notice these berries when I lived here? How festive they make the bushes! Perfectly round, the only color here, they're like bunches of tiny cherries stuck onto branches. Deeper in the woods, hundreds of them dance on high branches like red stars against the dark trees.

I hear a pickup truck behind me; evidently it has come up the nearly impassable road from Delaware Water Gap. The driver waves. Twenty yards beyond me he stops suddenly and jumps out. He trots over, lightly grabs my arm, and pulls me toward the woods.

"Did you see it?" he asks, pointing into the swamp. "There! It's just standing there. Albino."

Indeed, deep in the woods I can just make out a white deer.

"I've seen it two or three times now," the man says. We stand together staring until the animal moves off.

I continue my walk, heading into the fields and then along trails through oak and birch and pine. As I walk on an old trail past a stand of four big Scotch pines, an explosion by my right ear startles me. A ruffed grouse, Pennsylvania's state bird, has once again flapped away so suddenly and noisily it seems the branches themselves have exploded into flight. *Explode* is the right word—it seems as if half the tree detonates. I wonder why the birds always let you get so close, like boys itching to light firecrackers beside you.

I purposely walk by a hill thick with Scotch pines, but see no more grouse. I get another unexpected sensation though. My feet sink into a patch of moss as if it were plush carpet, my whole body lowering at least an inch. It makes me want to lie down in the moss and look up at the sky.

My mind is on God's surprises. Sometimes they explode into our lives like a ruffed grouse. Other times things happen to us and we squint into the woods, searching and wondering if it really is an albino or just the trunk of a white birch.

Surprises!

The earth is a bizarre, alluring, terrible, beautiful place, and its Creator answers prayer on his own terms.

Including surprises!

Scripture is full of them.

"Say, Noah, build an ark. I'm going to flood the world."

Quite a surprise!

We're told Christ will come "like a thief in the night." Watch out! Surprises good and bad are coming. Which do we get? Depends. . . .

Jesus tells a story about a boss away and the people play. They do selfish things; then the boss comes back.
Surprise! Payday!

Is your lamp trimmed? Watch out! The bridegroom's back!

Suddenly there's a burning bush out in the desert. Watch out, Moses! This will lead to more surprises—bloody plagues, millions of frogs, and forty years of tramping around a desert. But it will also bring the Ten Commandments and the glory of God glowing on you so brightly people are blinded by it.

"We live by God's surprises," said Helmut Thielicke, speaking not from some safe little Sunday school class but standing in his half-bombed-out church in World-War-II Germany, knowing he and his war-ravaged listeners might have to run for shelter any minute at the next wave of allied bombers.

"God packs our lives with surprises all the time," said the tough-minded debunker Oswald Chambers who, despite wanting a career in the arts, ended up preaching out of a tent in World War I. He both warned and promised that we have to be ready for God's "surprise visits" all the time.

God's surprises. The phrase conjures up miracles and blessings and marvelous rescues from terrible events. But there is another side that's considerably less attractive, and that is that God also sends his surprises through pain.

Why must life be so maddeningly haphazard, so unstable, about to shift any moment?

I'm at the table again, surrounded by books and photos from the past, writing on a yellow pad.

Surprises. In childhood, we were always ready for the good surprises. We were like sea creatures with cilia wavering everywhere to detect a morsel of excitement.

All those wonderful firsts were surprises. The first sight of a bird startled into flight. The first puppy nuzzling our necks. The first time we saw a marching band leading a parade.

I remember the moment I fed my infant daughter her first spoonful of ice cream. We were sitting in a Big Boy restaurant, and Michelle's little face suddenly came vividly alive with excitement and pleasure. All the mashed carrots and beef puree paled before this utterly alien, *wonderful* new taste. Childhood has so many good surprises: feeling those first gentle raindrops on our faces, seeing fireworks with new eyes, touching our first snow, or lifting off in an airplane the first time.

But then there are others. The first hot stove. The first humiliation. The first bully. The first realization that life's surprises are a mixture of wonderful things, ordinary things—and terrible things.

My son Todd started kindergarten full of enthusiasm, backed by years of security and happiness in our family and nursery school. Photos of him at three and four show him smiling broadly in Oshkosh overalls or peering joyously from under me as he crawls "under the bridge." Then came the great jolt: the harsh environment of hostile peers shoved him into the cruel realities of the schoolyard, and for a time Todd smiled very little.

Bad surprises. Good surprises. The rain falls on the just and the unjust. Who gets the good? Who gets the bad?

In Chicago a few years ago, I saw David Bowie—of all people—play the part of the Elephant Man, John Merrick. At the play's beginning the actor stood before us, muscular, energetic, controlled. Then the actual photos of the hideously deformed Merrick, who died in England in 1890, appeared on a screen behind Bowie. As each slide was projected, the actor stiffened into more and more grotesque positions, symbolically projecting the anguish of the man in those photos: huge misshapen head, tumors over most of his distorted body, so ugly he would wear a sack over his head and become known as "the elephant man."

The play told the story of John Merrick, a man with the soul of an artist, who was vilified as a sideshow freak. Finally befriended by a doctor and protected by England's royalty, this man known as "nature's disgrace" built an exquisite scale model of a cathedral that can be viewed in London today.

Long, long after the play was over, one word lingered in my mind.

Merrick was amazed at life's capriciousness, at the tragic quirk that had made him suffer. In discussing the plight of others in tragic circumstances, someone told him that life was "chancy." On hearing that, Merrick cried out like a pierced animal. "Chancy!" The word rang through the theater. "Chancy!" It ripped out of his throat again, even more loudly and brokenly, crying his bewilderment at the intolerable truth. "Chancy!"

Chancy indeed. Showers of unexpected events pour on us all our lives. Who gets the good? Who can tell? A remarkable thing is how it's all turned on its head. Most of us would like fame and fortune, but what in the long run did it do for Elvis Presley or Rick Nelson or John Belushi, now dead because of it? Or look at the lottery winners who thought their jackpots were the best of all possible surprises but who now say the money wrecked their lives.

In Monopoly you land on Chance and you draw a good card or a bad card. But in life itself, good might be bad, or bad good. David Merrick's grotesque afflictions ultimately brought him friendship with the queen. Auschwitz—that horrendous evil—even Auschwitz had its Father Kolbe resisting the evil and giving his life for his fellow prisoners. And the icy Gulag had Solzhenitsyn chronicling its despair and hope, showing incredible faith in the midst of horror, and, unthinkably, thanking God for prison.

Good surprises. Bad surprises. Which is which, and who's behind them?

~

A pipeline as wide as a four-lane highway cuts a swath through the woods of Kittatinny Mountain and through the fields by my parents' home. I walk on it in fields where corn and timothy hay once grew; now small trees and bushes spot each side of the pipeline. Far below I see what I think is a rabbit, then realize it is an ordinary gray housecat, crouched, intent. Soon I hear deer in the woods and it becomes clear that the cat is actually stalking them. I early laugh aloud, wondering what the cat would do with a deer if it caught one.

The cat moves toward the deer, ears cocked, stopping every few seconds, muscles tensing at each rustling. Suddenly the cat sees me and freezes. I stand motionless and it stares at me, trying to figure out what I am. Finally I say softly, "Here, kitty, kitty, kitty!" Instantly it bounds off.

Near where the cat was crouched stands a tall, slender tree with plum-size red fruit. It looks like a pear tree, but the fruit, shriveled by the November cold, resembles large cherries. A mystery. The tree is young, yet no one has tended these fields in thirty years. Did someone toss some old fruit here fifteen years ago? I pick one and squeeze it between my fingers. Little seeds inside; looks edible. Most of the fruit is at the very top of the tree, as if someone had climbed a high ladder and decorated it.

The tree is loaded with little red Christmas balls. Do elves live here?

I get more "Christmas" a few yards away. Clusters of the same round, red berries intertwine with the branches of a tall cedar—the classic holiday shades of red and green here in the woods. Generous clumps of white berries cling to another bush close by, and the cedar itself is covered with thousands of tiny, light blue berries. I pick one and roll it between my fingers. The blue rubs off, like paint. Growing on low bushes nearby are oval red berries and dull black ones.

Am I really seeing all these colors in one spot, this Christmas without tinsel? I've often walked by these trees and bushes and seen nothing.

Surprises are everywhere. But most of the time we have to be out looking for them.

God's surprises. In small events and pivotal moments. Christmas where we don't expect it; humor in a chancy world. Are we kidding ourselves to think God is in charge? Or does our connection with him give us new sight?

We see "through a glass darkly," but we do see more than mere chance.

Thielicke was a man penetratingly aware of tragedy. He would have fully understood the elephant man's cry, "Chancy!" When Thielicke said, "We live by God's surprises," he had personally suffered under the Nazis. As a pastor he wrote to young soldiers about to die; he comforted mothers and fathers and children after the bombs killed their loved ones. He preached magnificent sermons week after week as bombs blew apart his church and the lives and dreams of his parishioners. He spoke of God not only looking in love at his suffering people, weeping with them as they were surrounded by flames, but of God's hand reaching into the flames to help them, his own hand scorched by the fires.

From the depths of suffering and the wanton destruction during the Nazi regime, Thielicke held out a powerful Christian hope. To Germans disillusioned by the easily manipulated faith of their fathers, he quoted Peter Wust: "The great things happen to those who pray. But we learn to pray best in suffering."

Prayer, suffering, joy, and the surprises of God. They are all tightly enmeshed. But most shrink from Peter Wust's statement, seeing suffering as the surest killer of both joy and "great things."

Oswald Chambers was equally aware of the agonizing, maddening "riddle" of a universe in which loved ones die and easy religious answers evaporate. He more than once quoted these phrases from Tennyson which resonated with his own experience:

Life is not as idle ore,
But iron dug from central gloom,
And heated hot with burning fears.
And dip't in baths of hissing tears,
And batter'd with the shocks of doom
To shape and use.

Chambers was a sharp-eyed realist about the sorrows and tedium of life, yet in describing God's surprises he became passionately enthusiastic: "The element of surprise," he said, "is always the note of the Holy Ghost in us. We are born again by the great surprise—'The wind bloweth where it listeth, and thou hearest the voice thereof, but knoweth not whence it cometh, and whither it goeth: so is everyone that is born of the Spirit.' Men cannot tie up the wind; it blows where it lists; neither can the work of the Holy Spirit be tied up in logical methods. Jesus never comes where we expect him; if he did, he would not have said, 'Watch.' Be ye also ready: for in an hour that ye think not the son of man cometh.[1] Jesus appears in the most illogical connections, where we least expect him, and the only way [you] can keep true to God is to be ready for his surprise visits. . . . It is this intense reality of expecting him at every turn that gives life the attitude of child wonder that Jesus wants it to have. When we are rightly related to God, life is full of joyful uncertainty and expectancy—we do not know what God is going to do next; he packs our lives with surprises all the time."

What a strange idea: "Joyful uncertainty." Most of us view uncertainty as cause for anxiety, not joy. Yet this call to expectancy rings true. The idea of standing on tiptoe to see what God is going to do next, even in the worst of circumstances, can transform our way of seeing. Prayer becomes the lens through which we begin to see from God's perspective.

This was true in Jesus' day too. The people prayed for deliverance, but most of them didn't have eyes to see the outrageous surprise God sent, for it shattered all their religious perceptions and expectations. They expected a messiah—yes, a Jewish king with the guts and power to defeat the Romans—not a carpenter who became an itinerant preacher and then got himself executed. They prayed for deliverance by a mighty leader. Instead, God left them with a handful of uneducated disciples.

~

I drive my father's old station wagon to Stroudsburg, less than ten minutes away, to get groceries and cards from a Hallmark shop for Jeanette and the kids. A block off Main Street is the courthouse square where old Dr. Marshall Metzgar treated, it seemed, everyone in Monroe County. He delivered thousands of babies, most of them at home. He slept on our couch on the bad nights when my grandmother lay dying but charged so little we wondered how he stayed in business. He died in his nineties.

Dr. Metzgar's office was a stone's throw from the imposing courthouse with its pillars rising above the park square in front of it. The jail to the right of the park is like a shabby relative, almost out of sight, almost out of mind.

Except to some of us. This is where Richie awaited trial after they caught him in Florida.

But this is also where some of us came to hold services on Sunday afternoons. We'd sing and testify while the glum-faced prisoners put up with us. To most of them we were simply a diversion from their boredom. I never saw a response.

Except once.

That day we had brought a guitar and an amplifier. We plugged it in and sang some gospel songs. Then the amp shorted out and stopped us flat. The wire was in a puddle of water on the concrete floor, so we moved it, checked the connection, and got it going again. After a couple more verses, it shorted out again.

We were embarrassed and glad to hand the program off to our pastor, who started preaching. Before he had completed his first major point, a bleary-eyed, balding prisoner obviously still under the influence said, "That's right, preacher, you tell 'em! I know what you're saying is true, 'cause I saw a woman raised from the dead in Pittsburgh! Yessir, saw 'er raised from the dead myself."

Our pastor didn't try to respond. He just nodded at the man and went on preaching. But the one-man cheering squad kept affirming his message, telling about other miraculous events. "I've seen miracles! Lots of 'em!"

Our credibility at that moment seemed about as great as the strange prisoner's. We felt embarrassed as the pastor valiantly kept preaching and finally closed with an invitation to receive Christ.

I don't know if I was ever more surprised in my life. Three men responded almost immediately and stayed for counseling. And as if to stamp the event in all our minds, two of the men began attending our church after their release.

As Chambers says, God appears in the most illogical connections and when we least expect him. And sometimes his surprises come right out of the heart of our weaknesses—with an edge of humor. If we have eyes to see.

4
LIVING BY PERSISTENCE

I'm on the ridge a half mile behind our house, hesitating about taking a newly discovered trail. It goes steeply downhill, probably a couple miles all the way to Cherry Valley Road. I start down, and within minutes, much sooner than I expected, I'm at the base of the hill.

Before me is a long driveway with a perfect row of stately cedars on each side. In the haphazard forest, the symmetry seems displaced, making me feel as if I've wandered into a French landscape painting. Who planted these trees? Where does this drive go?

I follow it, and it ends at an old blacktop road. In a moment I recognize the spot and am taken aback. My sense of geography was all wrong. I thought I was lower and west, not here on Mountain Road high above the village. Interesting how one can for decades picture reality and then, in a moment of truth, see its illusions.

Mountain Road is half the width it was when we rode over it in the school bus. Moss grows out of the aged asphalt and winter ice has created wide patches of loose stones. I remember well the fresh black tar when the road was laid thirty years ago; it was a wonder of a road contrasted to the packed dirt that preceded it.

As I walk, I pass a familiar driveway now leading to an empty lot where a house once stood. Here a mother and her two children came from the city to live. The woman would not put up with a dirt road. She called the road department. She called every county official possible and demanded the road be paved. We thought her insistence was odd, but one day the trucks came. They paved from the country club up the steep hill and on past her house—a thick, wide, black, beautiful road. There the trucks stopped. The stretch from her house past ours remained dirt.

As the saying goes, the squeaky wheel gets the grease.

A half mile past our house in the other direction lived another determined woman. She not only made incessant phone calls about the dirt road, but also sent the county her cleaning bills when her clothes were splashed from the puddles. She persisted for years, and she finally got her blacktop road.

My parents never dreamed of doing the same thing, so our mile-and-a-half stretch of road between the two women's houses remained dirt.

As I walk along the road that was fought for but is now being reclaimed by time and weather, I find myself asking, "Is this how it is with prayer, Lord?" Thoughts not entirely welcome flow into my mind, all indicating, "Yes, it probably is."

The matters we deal with in prayer are often of far greater consequence than a paved road. Does that mean it requires even more effort than these women expended?

What an uncomfortable thought. Why should prayer be such an effort, such hard work? Jesus said, "He who seeks, finds. To him who knocks, it shall be opened." Sounds like a simple, warm invitation. But then Jesus also said, "Ye have not because ye ask not," which carries that jab of accusation.

Jesus, in teaching about prayer, told stories about intensely persistent people, as determined to get what they wanted as our two neighbors. He spoke of a widow who had been wronged. She demanded action from the judge. He put her off, but she kept pestering him. Although the judge feared neither God nor man, he wanted to get the widow off his back, so he finally gave her what she wanted.

Back at the house I look up the Bible story in Luke 18. After telling it, Jesus proclaimed in a ringing promise that if an unjust judge responds to persistence, "Will not God bring about justice for his chosen ones, who cry out to him day and night?"

A wonderful promise. Yet it's colored by Jesus' pessimistically adding: "However, when the Son of Man comes, will he find faith on the earth?"

The same kind of tension is evident after Jesus teaches his disciples the Lord's Prayer. He tells them the story about the man whose neighbor knocks on his door at midnight demanding bread for his overnight guests. The man tells the neighbor to go back home, but he keeps knocking, and finally the man gives him the bread. Jesus sums up the point of the story by saying, "Ask and it will be given to you; seek and you will find; knock and the door will be opened to you." Then, as if to drill it home, he repeats it. "For everyone who asks receives; he who seeks finds; and to him who knocks, the door will be opened."

Jesus often used unpleasant people in his stories, contrasting their character with God's, and he seemed incredulous that his disciples didn't understand. Surely the Father in heaven "gives good gifts to his children," he told them. "Would you give your child a scorpion if he asked for an egg, or a snake if he asked for a fish?"

Well, sometimes it would seem so. Bitter tragedies tear apart praying people as well as pagans. We all know that, and it was Jesus himself who pointed out that the rain falls on the just and the unjust. Despite that, he made vigorous, pointed promises about the certainty of God answering prayer.

In reality, Jesus dumps it all in our laps. If we want it, we can get it. Just ask, he says—constantly, persistently. This is the part that makes us uncomfortable. Are we to be like nagging children with God? Not a pleasant picture, nor is the guilt of wondering if we are to be so self-disciplined that we go through life on our knees, "praying without ceasing." Do we have to chase it all the time, like an Olympic athlete who "wants it so bad he can taste it"?

This sports analogy reminds me of something Rick Christian said in his book *Alive.* "When in training for my college rowing team, I couldn't let up. Six days a week my alarm would ring at 4:30 A.M. Whether I felt like it or not, I'd drag myself out of bed and into my sweats. Breakfast was two raw eggs smooshed together in a glass of orange juice and guzzled on my way out the door.

"Headlights of my old Chevy Nova cut a swath of brightness in the black, pre-dawn day as I headed for the boathouse for a two-hour workout before classes. After each workout, I'd be soaked with sweat, and there were many times when my hands would be raw and bloody from the constant twisting and rubbing of the oar. The salt water of the bay stung my palms with pain—until my eyes welled up with tears.

"Sometimes I'd sit in the locker room after practice and think I must be crazy to keep up with this. But I didn't quit because I knew it took that kind of work and determination to meet my athletic goals.

"However, I sometimes feel a certain guilt in knowing I have not often set and pursued spiritual goals with the same relentless work and determination."

Probably Jesus would endorse Rick's analogy, no matter how uncomfortable it makes me, for Jesus told stories of highly determined people, then linked them to his teachings about prayer. It seems clear that he meant we should be just as determined and just as expectant as Rick working out on the oars at dawn or the widow and the neighbor who refused to give up. Jesus "plays hardball" here. It was he, after all, who said that the great commandment is "love the Lord your God with all your hearts, all your souls, all your minds."

Bestselling author Scott Peck in *The Road Less Traveled* also writes about the importance of persistence as he's experienced it. Although intelligent and well-educated, Peck always considered himself "a mechanical idiot." One day he told a neighbor who was fixing a lawn mower that he was unable to fix things. The neighbor shot back, "That's because you don't take the time." The comment stayed with him. Later he did take the time, and actually found he could fix something. His neighbor was right, says Peck. It's easy to throw up our hands about life's tougher demands and say, "It's beyond me!"

How easy it is to feel that way about prayer, too—that others are "natural pray-ers" but we're not.

Although Scott Peck still does not "fix things" as a rule, he knows when he doesn't he's making a priority choice. Other things are more important to him. When we pray or fail to pray, we are doing the same thing. The objective test of the importance of prayer in our lives is: What do I *do?*

And part of the reason we so often relegate prayer to the fringe of our lives has to do with our conflicting, ambivalent beliefs about it.

We read Tennyson's statement on a wall poster, "More things are wrought by prayer than this world dreams of," and we anticipate powerful answers. We read, "The fervent prayer of a righteous man availeth much," and then life seems to contradict that statement. We find no conclusive proof that prayer "works" in a magical sense. When we pray about someone whose marriage is breaking up, or for a loved one who is an alcoholic, or for someone with cancer, life and consequences usually march on without miraculous intervention. We wonder if this "talking to ourselves" really makes any difference.

Some time ago I was watching a movie on television about a man going through deep troubles. One scene has stayed in my mind. The man is in a hotel room, discouraged, facing insuperable difficulties. He looks across the street and there, on a sign affixed to a rescue mission, flashes the message, "Prayer Changes Things." The man makes no comment nor does his expression change, giving the viewer the impression that the sign is irrelevant, a strange artifact. Nothing will change. The filmmaker apparently had no understanding of the fact that prayer changes everything.

First of all, it changes us.

Norwegian theologian O. Hallesby labels prayers that simply ask God for something as "pagan," and he indicates we all have enough of the pagan in us to pray that way. Prayer is not even remotely like phoning orders in to an eternal bellhop; instead it is getting ourselves into the flow of God's purposes. But when our pagan prayers aren't answered, we think God has ignored us. Then we take things into our own hands, seeking more practical remedies.

Our beliefs are also flavored by our culture's caricatures of people who pray. None of us want to be seen as sanctimonious wimps with calloused knees and calloused hearts, oblivious to people's real needs. The caricature is false of course. True prayer inevitably leads the pray-er to help others. But that does not limit such depictions from springing to life on movie and television screens. There, those few characters who do pray are usually shown as hypocrites or nerds. These images powerfully affect us, no matter how much we discount them.

However, even if we saturate our minds with Scripture and biblically sound writings, it's still difficult to find time to pray in our fast-paced world. This is not a cop-out; all of us struggle with the limitations of time. The sincere Christian faces rather quickly an array of tasks no one human can possibly do. Economics is called "the dismal science" because there is never enough to go around; it is the same with time. For many, it is an exercise in futility to try to establish a time budget that includes school or work, church, family responsibilities, civic duties—just knowing the political candidates and what they stand for is an awesome task, if taken seriously! And the list of imperatives goes on and on. It is ironic that sermons calling for more dedication, including the need for more prayer, are usually directed at those who already pummel their consciences daily and try the hardest.

But when Jesus talks about persistence in prayer, he is not laying on the guilt. He's saying, "Here's good news for you." Like a coach who says, "You can do it! You can win! But there's a price."

Jesus said the Sabbath was made for man, not the other way around. In other words, the day of rest was to nourish people and bring them alive in God's grace and love. Prayer was made for man, too—like air and food and sex. It is essential. But unlike the physical necessities, prayer can be ignored. When we do that, we ignore God's invitation to life itself.

It's another of those paradoxes that permeate life. There is a price to be paid, based on a universal principle: giving the best to God. The Old Testament commandment to give God the firstfruits and the best of the crops and herds parallels Jesus' words to Mary and Martha. Although the household arrangements had to be made, Jesus tells Mary she has chosen rightly in spending her time with him instead of the dishes. Martha loses out. The dishes must be done, but they are not a priority—at least not when measured against time needed for spiritual things.

It may be hard to imagine Jesus as the tough coach of an Olympic team demanding total effort; yet his words carry that same hard, promising edge of reality. "Do this, not for me, but for the great rewards and opportunities that lie ahead."

As the old adage goes, the good is ever enemy of the best. It's struck me as interesting that both George MacDonald and Oswald Chambers insisted that morning is the prime time to meet God. Perhaps they were just morning people; or perhaps they were right. Either way, the message behind their insistence, it seems to me, is that God deserves our best time, not moments between the cracks when we are tired and distracted.

In research done for *Leadership* journal, those especially sensitive to the need for prayer—pastors—said they are often riddled with guilt about their lack of it. All the research I've come across says committed Christians admit they "don't pray enough." It's odd, in light of all the books, seminars and wall plaques.

Evangelist and theologian Charles Finney, who made one of the most remarkable spiritual impacts America has ever known, said that he could do nothing if he lost the spirit of prayer, and he advised a student: "I am convinced that nothing in the whole Christian religion is so difficult, and so rarely attained, as a praying heart. Without this you are as weak as weakness itself."

Finney summed up the dilemma: nothing so difficult, yet no opportunity so great.

Many other theologians have also recognized and voiced the difficulty; prayer is the source of pain and striving as well as joy. They give many reasons for this, including strategies of Satan, who at all costs would keep us from our most powerful weapon against evil. The fact is, the deeper we go in the Christian life, the more clearly we see evil's enormous power and the more we realize that only through prayer and God's Word can we stand against the darkness.

Through prayer we welcome in the mysterious forces of God's grace, forces more powerful than the most blatant evil.

"The great things happen to those who pray."

Martin Luther observed, "As it is the business of cobblers to make shoes, so it is the business of Christians to pray." And John Wesley said, "I am persuaded that God does everything by prayer, and nothing without it."

A few years ago Paul Robbins and I flew to Boston to interview Dr. Harold Ockenga. It was a cold, snowy, windy day in the Northeast, and Dr. Ockenga and his wife Audrey warmly hosted us in their home. What I recall most of that entire interview was our conversation about prayer and Dr. Ockenga's response.

"We hear a great deal these days about mid-life crisis," I said at one point. "Over all these decades of heavy ministry as pastor of Park Street Church and president of Fuller Seminary, did you ever experience anything like that?"

"I can't say that I have," he said without a pause.

I then asked how he was able to take so much weighty responsibility decade after decade. Was there ever a time when strife with people or the sheer volume of work brought him to a crisis?

"I have always been very busy," he said. "But there is a secret to that. You can do things okay if you keep a prayer list. I've kept one for forty-one years and have everything on that list. When I go over it, I'm reminded by the Lord if I haven't tried to solve a problem. . . . if I have enemies I'm praying for, something may come to my mind that I can do about that.

"Everything goes on my prayer list," Dr. Ockenga told us. "I write a brief summary of what the petition is, and I number and date it. When it's answered, I write across it, 'answered.' A few of them have been answered in the negative. I just put crosses right across those, and I know that they have been denied. This keeps a person alert to his responsibilities."

I responded that leaving things in God's hands releases one from anxiety.

"Yes," he said, "that's right. I never worry about it."

"How do you find time to pray?"

"I pray every morning. First I do my exercises, then shave and bathe, then pray until Audrey has breakfast ready. I pick up where I left off on my prayer list the day before. I've had this prayer habit since I was in college."

Harold Ockenga, who died a few years after the interview, had found prayer to be the key to his life.

More than once Billy Graham has told about one of his own personal experiences with Ockenga that left a deep impression. Their friendship began during the great Boston Crusade years ago. In some ways it was an odd association. Ockenga was an intellectual and pastor of a sophisticated congregation in historic Boston; Graham, with his warm Southern heritage, was a popular evangelist.

At the time, Graham happened to walk by Dr. Ockenga's office and saw him under the rug, of all things. Graham realized that Ockenga was in fervent prayer, wrestling with the Lord and was greatly moved. He later attributed much of the great spiritual fruit of that magnificent crusade to Harold Ockenga's prayers, and he was surely right.

But there is more to the story. Allan Emery, president of the Billy Graham Evangelistic Association and a longtime friend of both Graham and Ockenga, tells with great love and appreciation just what Dr. Ockenga was praying about under the rug. Dr. Ockenga had been instrumental in inviting Billy Graham to hold a New England crusade and worked energetically to help bring it about. Yet the limelight surrounding the evangelist caused him feelings of envy; Billy was doing in New England what he had not been able to do. He was under the rug that day pouring out those feelings to God.

Such emotions are common to all of us, but it is a mark of true saintliness that Harold Ockenga refused to give in to them; instead he poured them out before the Lord. Perhaps he had to be as persistent as the widow petitioning the judge—maybe his feelings resisted stubbornly. The important thing is that he prayed about them, even ended up under a rug over them. That's the sort of persistence Jesus answers—and answers in "great and mighty" ways. That's coming to God in weakness to be empowered, for who can possibly eradicate by one's own strength such sins as envy or anger or desire for power? But God can.

It is clear that God magnificently answered Harold Ockenga's prayers. He and Billy Graham made a remarkable team for decades, giving broad leadership to the evangelical movement not only through their own ministries, but through *Christianity Today,* the National Association of Evangelicals, and many other institutions.

What if, instead of praying that day for God's power, Harold Ockenga had coddled himself with self-pity, feeding his envy? Would Satan have used that to prevent future spiritual blessings?

The prayer under the rug made the future possible, releasing that powerful teamwork for the next decades.

"The great things happen to those who pray."

I look at my watch as I walk by Prosser's Lake. It's 4:30—sunset time, but charcoal gray skies obscure the sun. The only sign of its presence is a slate-colored ridge with bright peach fluff, like wild hair wisping away.

I pray for friends and colleagues and family as I walk, naming them one by one and envisioning God's grace flowing over their bodies like clean water or like sunshine pouring down on them, lifting their spirits. Someone once commented that he considered Paul's lists of people in the Epistles his favorite part of the Bible. I never could understand what he meant until I started praying for people, one by one, savoring their friendship and their unique persons, envisioning God's grace energizing them as his magnificent creatures.

I look up. The gray ridge has changed shape; now it's a volcano spewing up peach magma.

Remarkable. The sky, the world, they're never the same. If you're alert to the miracles of God, you never know, minute by minute, what you may find.

5
LIVING BY ADVENTURE

Despite a light rain and dripping leaves I am out on these old wagon trails again. I cannot resist them. Some are easy to detect; they are wagon-wide ruts cutting boulevards through the forest. Others stretch promisingly for a short walk but soon disappear—starting nowhere, ending nowhere. Years of rolling wheels behind straining horses hardened the ground; now there is nothing but grass, leaves, rocks, and moss on these ghostly roads wending through oak, maple, poplar, and pine.

It's seventy-four degrees and humid. Odd for November. The snow of a few days ago has melted and the remaining moisture drips from bare limbs. I'm wearing a T-shirt and jeans, but with a red knit cap to block the drips. Would I look like some odd red-and-white elf to those wagoners of a century ago?

As I clamber over the stone rows, I wonder about the people who worked so hard here, ripping rocks from the soil. They say the farmers' plows would find new rocks rising up every spring like a fresh crop. Men grunted thousands of them onto wagons, hauling them to the rows framing their fields. Some weighed hundreds of pounds. All through this national forest their stone rows still stand, marking ancient fields. My father and I once backed up a wagon-sized trailer to one of those rows and filled it with rocks for use in a concrete floor. After throwing hundreds into the trailer, we had barely disturbed the row.

What changes have come since those twelve-hour days of heavy labor when horses and wagons traveled these trails. Yesterday I picked up a folder in Delaware Water Gap; it pictured a 1908 Studebaker Electric which can be seen in the Switgart Museum in Huntington, Pennsylvania. With its open wood sides, it looks like a wagon on Model-T wheels, a wagon in need of a horse. I can visualize it bouncing along on rubber tires past these stone rows, harbinger of a mechanized society.

There's a sadness about our great progress; I sense it in these woods. Frontiers are gone; each tiny island has been charted; every star is on someone's computer. The world's wildlife has been catalogued, and specimens pack museums. It's all so tame. We look to space for adventure, but only moviemakers find civilizations and drama there now. Even "one giant leap for mankind" is history.

We long for the challenges of the past. All over the Poconos are signs and brochures about earlier days, sites to be visited. Louis L'Amour's novels can be found in every drugstore and K-Mart. How, living in today's world, can we satisfy the desire for adventure that churns in each of us?

It is an awesome notion that the Creator of galaxies and volcanos and plankton, the Maker who holds all molecules together, is the one who planted in us these adventure-seeking seeds. God himself whispers the challenge. But who has ears to hear? Who can sense the powerful forces at work in our ordinary lives? Who can face up to the kinds of exploits he calls us to?

Even those men who lived daily with Jesus were largely oblivious to the nature of the true spiritual adventures he offered them; they preferred their own challenges instead. The disciples saw Jesus' miracles and heard his parables; they participated in events millions would retell century after century. But the deeper meanings eluded them, like fleeting shadows in the woods.

In the Garden of Gethsemane spiritual conflicts massed about the disciples, building toward God's terrible but glorious events that would shake the universe. The adventure was beginning, but they were asleep.

Were they not like us, unaware of the stakes, unaware of the drama taking place around them? They were bone tired. Yes, Jesus had asked them to watch and pray with him for an hour, but how were they to know their prayers were crucial? Besides, they were tired. How could they pray when they were so sleepy?

Jesus woke them with a reprimand and exhorted them to pray. "Get up and pray," he said, "so that you will not fall into temptation."

A few yards away Jesus was sweating drops of blood in his prayer battle against the heart of evil, yet his disciples slowly sagged back into sleep.

How stunned they must have been when they were startled awake a second time and found their quiet resting place filled with an angry mob crying for their Master's death. The dark day had arrived, and they were sleeping! Jesus stood firm in all his power, fueled by his time of prayer. Shivering with fear and weakness, the disciples deserted him and fled. They had missed the opportunity to pray with Jesus; and they were powerless to stand against their own fear.

Like the disciples, we may long for God's challenges in our lives, but we may not be ready for the actual adventures when they come, for they are far from child's play! Even Jesus, praying in the garden, asked that the cup pass from him. And on the cross he cried out, "My God! My God! Why hast thou forsaken me?"

Like the disciples, we are asked to pray. But all we see is the daily humdrum. We wonder about other disciples asleep around us, not recognizing our own temptation to slumber.

Scripture tells us that at times God bursts into our lives with untamed energy, like the *ruach*—the Hebrew word for a powerful, unpredictable wind. It may be wild and disruptive, full of cool wind, torrential rain, or scorching sand, or it may blow with force enough to smash a brick building. In the Old Testament the *ruach* is often connected with the Holy Spirit, and the psalmist speaks of God "who maketh the *ruach* his messengers, his ministers a flaming fire."

Like the wind, God cannot be predicted as he moves upon his creation and in our lives. He shakes our religious ideas and breaks apart our brittle concepts, our neat categories and answers.

A part of us craves adventure. We want to respond to God's call, yet we do not always hear it or understand it. Sometimes he seems too silent, other times too forceful. He speaks in quiet chapels, but he also thunders from smoking and holy mountains.

I am walking a trail on a high ridge in the woods. Someone built a fire here weeks ago and left a stack of newspapers on the ground. The headline on one—a historical article—catches my eye: "Local Churches for Settlers and Indians." I squat and read that Monroe County's first church was a log structure in Shawnee in 1741. By 1752, it was replaced by a stone meeting house used by the Dutch Reformed, Presbyterians, Lutherans, and Baptists.

Now, here's something! The settlers, it states, built the church windows well above the heads of the parishioners "in case of surprise Indian attack during the worship services." Prudent people.

I wonder, as I continue down the steep trail, how many of us build high walls of safe religious ideas so none of those wild *ruach* arrows can penetrate and prick our consciences at worship. Who wants a holy God breaking through his defenses all the time?

Arrows. When I was fourteen, my brother and I went to see *Fort Ti,* a movie about soldiers and Indians fighting for control of Fort Ticonderoga. It had been filmed in Hollywood's latest invention, 3-D. I was only fourteen and couldn't wait to view this much-touted visual wonder. As we entered the theater, we were given cardboard glasses with red-and-green plastic lenses. At first it seemed much like other action films of the era, except perhaps that the Indians moving stealthily through the woods and the soldiers with muskets watching them projected out more boldly from the screen, while the forest trail appeared to wind deep into the picture.

But then came the moment I will never forget. Indians were attacking the fort and soldiers were firing back. The camera closed in on one warrior holding an arrow tipped thickly with black pitch. He touched fire to the arrow and the pitch blazed brightly. The Indian knelt on one knee, drew his bow all the way back—then very deliberately turned so that he was aiming that blazing arrow right into the audience. He held the bow taut for a second, then let fly!

A burning arrow flashing at your head in 3-D is decidedly different from any other moment at the movies! I found myself instantly, literally, under the seat. Sheepishly, I looked up and around. Others were just rising, too; everyone in the theater had ducked.

Sometimes we feel we're faithfully following God's call in our lives—living as best we can the adventure we find ourselves in—when suddenly arrows start flying at us from unexpected places. The darts may come from the very persons we have trusted to protect us. Then we find ourselves flat on the ground, taking any available cover. We're stunned. How could hurtful missiles come from those directions?

Such mysteries torment us. Are they God's arrows or the enemy's? Can such a distinction ever be made when the arrows are flying? Is God involved in these terrible things that happen to us? Surely he takes no pleasure in our grief and pain. In this extremely dangerous thing called life, does God still care?

Personally, using the *ruach* as a metaphor for God's work in our lives makes me uncomfortable. I feel much easier with an analogy like the deer stepping in and out of our lives with grace and mystery. I'd like my life interesting and lively, but not buffeted by the fierce *ruach.*

I love to read about J.R.R. Tolkien's hobbits, those little creatures who are such marvelous symbols of God's weak agents fighting evil and, through obedience, winning great battles. But I want to enjoy their gutsy adventures vicariously, settled down in my easy chair. Let them draw swords against dragons and trek over arid wastelands. Let them face giant spiders, battle horrible orcs, and face dark dens of monsters—as I sip a cold drink safely behind the pages.

But I cannot be just an observer. Real life is an adventure too, including evil and fear and dashed hopes. And when the hobbits wonder if their adventure is all poppycock; when they worry that Gandalf, who inspired it, might be wrong; when they fight among themselves, it is all too reminiscent of the dramas of my own life.

Our own adventures are as rewarding, tedious, frightening, and perplexing as those of the hobbits. Prayer does not take the bite out of them. In fact, it may do just the opposite. Writer Virginia Stem Owens describes prayer as going "into the Lion's jaws." She observes, "Awful things happen to people who pray. Their plans are frequently disrupted. They end up in strange places." When we invite God into our lives, all sorts of things can happen.

I read in a magazine once that at the start of the Civil War some young ladies in Washington, D.C., observed young men marching off to war in their dashing blue uniforms. They sensed an adventure was about to begin! They were told the armies were to clash not far away, so they set off in their fancy carriages with picnic lunches to enjoy the view. As they settled down on the grass to eat their lunch and observe the action, the battle suddenly came close enough for them to see much too well the effect of cannons on horseflesh and the awful way young men die. In a great panic, they fled in their carriages.

Perhaps we're a bit like that when we sing "Onward, Christian Soldiers," forgetting—or not even realizing—that spiritual adventure includes trench warfare, jungle leeches, lethargy, and the whole miserable discomfort of war.

I'm browsing in a Delaware Water Gap gift shop and notice a card with this classic verse: "And I said to the man who stood at the gate of the year, 'Give me a light that I may tread safely into the unknown.' And he replied, 'Go out into the darkness and put your hand into the hand of God. That shall be to you better than light and safer than the known way.'" A good bit of wisdom.

My eyes are drawn to something next, though, whose tone may fit even better the adventures most of us end up with. It's a big poster of a chimp with gum spread all over his hands and mouth. The caption exclaims, "Life is one sticky situation after another."

All of us are driven by complex forces we don't fully grasp, intricacies that amaze us and discourage us. Jay Kesler, president of Taylor University, commented to me one day, "You know, we're all a bit odd, a bit off center. If you rolled any one of us down a hill, we'd go bump, bump, bump!"

If we live with people, work with people, worship with people, life gets sticky indeed. We're told by Jesus to love one another, but we end up frustrating each other and wondering what God could possibly have had in mind when he put us together.

It takes a lot of prayer and humor to appreciate each other, a lot of God's grace to accept our companions in this adventure. We are shoved together, like it or not. And like hobbits and dwarves, we don't find it easy to make common cause against the enemy.

But the life we are living is the only adventure we have, and our companions aren't going to change. A cartoon from the *New Yorker* illustrates how we sometimes feel. It shows a man in a very long tunnel, sadly walking away from a distant, tiny square of light. The caption reads: "Discovering the light at the end of the tunnel is New Jersey."

New Jersey? The long-anticipated, longed-for, fought-for light is, of all things—*New Jersey?*

Obviously, this is a New York cartoonist's humor, but its implications are universal. We're all slogging through some sort of tunnel, hoping to see a light at the end of it; often it turns out to be more of the same, only worse.

I think of Eugene Petersen's wonderfully apt book

title, *A Long Obedience in the Same Direction.* A long obedience—even in drab, dusky tunnels.

Tedium. Discouragement. Outrageous acts. Betrayal! We are often stunned by the actions of those closest to us. In surveying pastors, *Leadership* journal has found that more than half have felt betrayed by someone they deeply trusted. Strangely enough, in most of these situations both parties feel betrayed: the wife by the husband, the husband by the wife; the pastor by the elder, the elder by the pastor. Each feels innocent; each feels the other did the betraying.

This is the sort of thing that makes up adventures—if we could but see it. When amid fervent prayer the Holy Spirit moves like the *ruach* into our lives and reveals realities about ourselves, we participate in the real warfare. These are the times God's grace can transform pain into love. There is not always reconciliation, but there is always God at work.

Several years ago someone decided to sue Christianity Today, Inc. for a huge sum of money. It was an absurd, maddening lawsuit. However, in the United States anyone can sue anyone if he can find a lawyer to work on contingency. Attorneys marched into our offices, demanding to see our files; they copied thousands of letters, not one of which had a line of incriminating evidence. At Christmastime, I found myself in a courtroom hundreds of miles from home watching lawyers haul large boxes of "evidence" before the judge and make "conspiracy" allegations. To defend ourselves, we were forced to spend more than a quarter million dollars on attorneys and other costs.

"Why does God allow this?" I wondered. "What a waste of energies and funds!"

While filled with such questions, I happened to watch a PBS television program on the fall of Poland in World

War II. The carnage was terrible! Warsaw was nearly leveled, paving the way for the slaughter of the Polish Jews. Entire families were destroyed. "There was evil everywhere," I thought, "and evil won." The Poles, on horseback with muskets, charged the machines of modern warfare and were mown down. Evil won the day.

Eventually, of course, Hitler was thrust back, but Stalin—who killed millions of innocents—was not. And Warsaw is now ruled by those who attack faith and impose their will with the sword.

Yet in the midst of all that did not the believers in Poland call out to God to save them and their precious families? Did not the Jews cry out to the God of their fathers for mercy? Does not the church in Poland today plead with heaven for deliverance?

I realized, watching the slaughter of the Poles, that I could pray mightily against evil, but evil might still win. The lawsuit against CTi seemed a destructive bombardment built on lies; but if a jury's emotions were swayed, their decision would say to the world we were guilty of something we had never even contemplated.

As I wrestled with all this I was intrigued by an Oswald Chambers comment I came across, where he said that God is curiously abrupt with programs and takes delight in breaking them up.

Does God build something like this up, then tear down? I wondered. Why? And what about my own reputation? Should I be anxious for it?

The questions boiled down to this: Was I willing to be made holy? Powerful spiritual forces were at work. If I could be disturbed at the prospect of my work and reputation being destroyed, was I truly at peace with God?

During the lawsuit, the spiritual battle drove all of us at CTi to our knees. I think the greatest weight we felt was our responsibility for ground God had placed under our feet and expected us to hold through prayer for we recalled marvelous past events that had seemed amazingly providential.

At that time, I came across a story about Saint Ignatius of Loyola. When asked what he would do if someone moved against the order to which he had devoted his life, Ignatius answered that he would pray about it for fifteen minutes and then wouldn't think of it again. We quoted his statement to each other as a challenge to hold lightly whatever God put into our hands.

I also found the words of Thomas à Kempis fascinatingly apt for this occasion: "It is good for us that at times we have sorrows and adversities . . . it is good that at times we endure opposition, and that we are evilly and untruly judged when our actions and intentions are good . . . for then we seek God's witness in the heart."

When the lawsuit was over, we sensed God had worked not only in the courts but in our souls. "The results to CTi and all of us," I wrote in my journal, "have been a great deepening of our prayer lives and our corporate roles being placed before Him. The lawsuit made us go to the depth of the question. 'What if God took all this away from us and instead gave humiliation?' I came to see that this was God's problem. Poverty, failure, grief—we accept them from God's hand. The new year lies ahead, full of opportunities and dangers."

It's night time. I'm sitting in my dad's big chair reading *Dragonflight* by Anne McCaffrey. A dozen other fantasy, science fiction, and classic fairy tales are stacked on the floor beside me. I'm writing some fantasy books for children, so I'm immersing myself in all sorts of strange stories of other worlds and other realities.

Oddly enough, though, the other-worldly idea that intrigues me most is a statement I read yesterday in a Peter Marshall sermon:

There is an air of reality about the gospel.
It is not a fairy tale in which Cinderella's rags
are changed into the robes of a queen,
but rather a promise in which Cinderella in her rags
becomes more queenly.

I love the thought. My mind spins it away in a fantasy story that keeps me scribbling ideas in between my reading of other books. It does all that because of a spiritual reality that *Dragonflight* and *Dragon's Egg* and a host of books do not have.

God is at the heart of all true adventures. His universe is vast enough to contain more remarkable stories than anyone could count or imagine. Behind all creativity is "the Father of lights"; yet he is also Father to you and me in each of our life stories.

When Bilbo is reviewing all his adventures at the end of *The Hobbit,* the good wizard Gandalf observes, "You don't really suppose, do you, that all your adventures . . . were managed by mere luck, just for your sole benefit? You are a very fine person, Mr. Baggins, and I am very fond of you, but you are only quite a little fellow in a wide world after all."

To which Bilbo replied, laughing, "Thank goodness."

Maybe we can learn from that—we who are little ones indeed. The adventure lies in being *God's* little ones.

6
LIVING BY FAITH

Dressed warmly against the raw wind and drizzle, I turn left at the big lilac bush at the bottom of the driveway and start walking toward the Gap. I look up through the specks of rain on my glasses and see a man plowing toward me through the wind and wet. I thought I was the only one foolish enough to take a walk in this weather.

The man is Mr. Siegfried, the owner of the barn that burned down last week. The Siegfrieds were foster parents to Richie's sisters. There were five children in the family. My parents had Richie, Royal, and Margie; the Siegfrieds had Debbie and Sharon. After a brief conversation, Mr. Siegfried continues on toward his house and the still-smoldering barn.

As I walk in the opposite direction, I think of Richie

and his brothers and sisters, five precious little kids for whom the state had to intervene. I think of the children two doors up the hill from the Siegfrieds, the ones who might have died last week if the kitty litter had caught fire.

When I was a little boy, we sang trustingly in Sunday school:

Jesus loves the little children,
All the children of the world.
Red and yellow, black and white,
They are precious in his sight.
Jesus loves the little children of the world.

I think of that famous anecdote about theologian Karl Barth, who when asked for the core of what he'd learned, simply recited:

Jesus loves me, this I know,
For the Bible tells me so.

Both these wonderful children's verses hold profound truths. Scripture even says, "God is love." Yet this revealed truth is not what we see in daily life where our experiences seem to say just the opposite.

The eloquently simple "Jesus Loves Me" includes the line: "Little ones to him belong; they are weak, but he is strong." If Jesus is strong, does that mean he will protect the weak little ones? It would seem not. Believing parents of dying children storm heaven with their prayers, but their children die anyway, as the doctors predict. Millions more pray for the starving, diseased, and abused children of the world, but the statistics remain grim.

Through my mind pass the faces of one wonderful child after another. Each was prayed for by loving parents; each died. In our small church alone, many have lost children, including our pastor. I think of the lovely girl on the street behind us who died of leukemia. I pray for friends all over the country who still grieve for lost children.

One day I was attending a meeting of pastors' wives where Jill Briscoe was speaking. In the course of the service Jill asked how many had lost children. I was shocked when nearly two dozen out of about 150 raised their hands. Surely these godly women had prayed fervently for their children's lives.

When Elsbeth lay dying, her heart was breaking for her two little boys and for Karba, her adopted African daughter. Karba had been born far out in the bush country of Nigeria. She was an eighth child, and in her tribe every eighth child was considered cursed and was left out on the rocks to die. A Christian chief had found Karba and rescued her; Elsbeth had then adopted her. Now Elsbeth was dying, unable to help her vulnerable child.

At first Elsbeth and David prayed for healing. Later, near the end of her life, Elsbeth cried out, "God! God! God!" and prayed, "Jesus Christ, help me! Help me! Help me believe you understand!"

We look at God's creation and cannot miss our Maker's magnificence and power, but his creation gives no evidence that he loves the little ones. Nature does not nurture the young; instead, it produces them in great numbers so that a few will survive.

In *Pilgrim at Tinker Creek,* Annie Dillard writes about "fecundity," graphically describing the extravagance of nature, the billions of eggs and larvae and offspring of all sorts. In nature, she says, life is "astonishingly cheap," and for all her intense and poetic love of God's creation, Dillard finds this fecundity appalling.

PBS aired a film on turtles some time ago. In it we saw eggs hatching on a beach, cute baby turtles rushing for the sea, and birds waiting to scoop most of them up before they reached the safety of the water. So it is with this planet's creatures. Millions of sperm to fertilize one egg. Millions of eggs eaten before they can hatch. Millions of babies providing tasty morsels for predatory creatures.

Says Dillard, "We value the individual supremely, and nature values him not a whit." She also says, "It is death that is spinning the globe."

Precisely. With all this astounding fecundity in animals and insects—and humans as well—it takes death, death, and more death to keep a few of us alive.

Like turtles racing for the sea, we are exposed to death every day. As Pascal said, a draft of air can kill you.

I am reminded of another PBS program I watched with my son Greg, a program about seals. We saw seals come to their breeding islands, bobbing in the water like scores of disembodied, whiskered heads. They awkwardly flippered ashore and commenced with an ecstatic party, wrestling, flopping about, like humans at a family reunion. The males acted like fools courting the females and eventually fought viciously for the right to mate gracefully in the water. Pups were born; mothers adored them, caressed them, suckled them.

However, the cameras also captured poignant scenes of lost pups. One lost its mother, and the mother seal searched the breeding ground for her baby. But most of the lost pups were never found. One adorable but doomed baby tried pathetically to suckle the body of another pup, not realizing it was dead.

Greg asked with indignation, "Why don't they feed it?" Yes, why didn't they? The watching humans filming the scene could have intervened; they had the power.

But that was not in their plan. They were there for "a greater purpose"—to photograph and record seal life as it really is. Who is to say, therefore, that they should have rescued the pups from starvation, pups that had been dying for millennia on the same islands, and would continue to die long after the camera crews were gone. The seal pups could not know about this greater purpose, of course; they were incapable of knowing or understanding why the humans were there.

The analogy is too obvious perhaps, but it stays with me. God has the same life-and-death power as those photographers, on a much grander scale. As we look up at him and wonder about his plan—thoroughly unreadable by us—we can only trust that he has "a greater purpose."

It's hard to watch seal pups starve. It's harder to watch children die.

~

It's Sunday. I hear odd sounds in the distance, as if someone's hitting a two-by-four against a tree. Whap! Whap! Whap!

I step outside. It's gunfire, probably half a mile away, shot after shot after shot, about one a second. Must be coming from a rifle range nearby.

It's a beautiful day, so I walk the mile loop on the road to where the Dolacks once lived. Everything was leveled by bulldozers when the federal government bought their land. I can't find a trace of the home the Dolacks built themselves, picking thousands of big, round fieldstones by hand and hauling them laboriously by wheelbarrow. I can still see old Joe and Ella in overalls, slapping concrete around the stones. It took them years to finish that house, their pride and joy. On the kitchen cabinets and trim their daughter painted Pennsylvania Dutch farmers and roosters and hex signs.

Joe Dolack was a big, quiet, gentle man. Once he had a puppy that got distemper and Ella complained he was too softhearted to shoot it. I said I'd do it for him.

Joe went with me out to a far stone row. "Does it have to be right now?" he asked when we stopped. At that moment it seemed I was the man and he was the tender-hearted kid. I wished I hadn't let him come with me. The necessary deed was done, but I don't think Joe ever felt I'd done him a favor.

That fall they learned Joe had cancer, and he was dead by Christmas.

I walk back through the fields Johnny and I crossed on the way to the school bus, climbing over the stone row near our house. This is the spot where, as a boy, I heard the rabbit scream. It was being chased by a weasel, and I watched it scramble over the stones with the little predator close behind; light brown and orange brown flashes of drama as the rabbit dove into a hole in the rocks and the weasel followed, hot after him. That's when I heard the terrible scream; it ripped through my body like slashing ice. I'd never heard such a sound, though I'd raised rabbits and handled frightened ones. I'd hunted rabbits and butchered dozens in a day for meat, but they had always been silent. The death scream of that wild rabbit stayed in my mind for days.

Past the remains of my rabbit hutches I spy what's left of the old shed. A male and female mallard roosted on it nightly one year. Before going to bed, we'd often look out at them sitting side by side on the roof ridge, outlined by the moonlight. Then one morning we found the drake sorrowfully circling the beheaded body of its mate. We figured an owl or hawk or maybe a weasel had killed it.

If ever I begin to wonder whether animals feel sorrow, I only have to recall that drake mourning its dead mate, humanlike in its circling grief.

I step into our backyard. All the time I've been exploring and reminiscing, the shooters have continued firing.

A mile away casings must be scattered in heaps on the ground. People take their guns seriously here; they aren't toys, carelessly handled. Johnny has rafters lined with pistols, rifles on the walls and in gun racks. He loads his own cartridges and wins matches in state competitions. Back in my days in the Marine Corps I took great pride in my own marksmanship, shooting expert on the rifle range with an M-1.

During my childhood here I sang "Jesus loves the little children; all the children of the world. Red and yellow, black and white, they are precious in his sight."

Now I read a *Time* cover story describing the children of war around the world . . . Belfast . . . Cambodia . . . Vietnam . . . Central America. . . . I listen to a missionary at our church tell of the terror the children of Uganda experienced during Idi Amin's reign and how even today, sitting in church schools, these children are unable to cope, their minds still fixed on those years of horror. In country after country throughout the world, soldiers deliberately destroy children as they attempt to "pacify" villages.

After World War II many German Lutherans felt their Christian doctrines had been ripped from their hearts. Thielicke quoted some church leaders who said: "After Auschwitz, the hymn verse 'who o'er all things so wondrously reigneth' cannot be sung."

As Thielicke preached to his parishioners in Hamburg, he understood well what had disillusioned these clergymen. He also knew why the young widows and orphans and grieving parents before him doubted the existence of a heavenly Father. In one sermon he quoted Jean Paul's "Death of God" vision: "The dead children awake in their little graves and ask the Son of God, 'Jesus, have we no Father?' And Jesus answers with streaming tears, 'We are all orphans, you and I; we are without a Father.'" This terrible vision depicts Jesus admitting that he was wrong, that there is no one. There is only "the numb, silent night," only "cold, eternal necessity," only "crazy chance."

Thielicke then asked his congregation, "Which one of us dares say a word against this honest despair? . . . The theoretical arguments which could be marshalled over against this vision of the void seem to stick in one's throat."

This loving pastor had heard members of his congregation praying fervently for years for husbands, fathers, and sons; yet many had never returned from battle. Their children had been killed in the bombings and many had felt the despair of "crazy chance" snuffing out their dearest hopes. To these families in the pews before him it did not seem God loved the little children of the world—or anyone else.

With eloquence, Thielicke spoke to their disillusionment. Through powerful exposition of the Scriptures he showed them "how to believe again." He challenged his parishioners to "take a chance with him who can call for graves to open and dead eyes to see."

Earlier, during the war itself, Thielicke had preached a series of messages on the Lord's Supper to his congregation in Stuttgart "who continued to assemble throughout the horrors of the air raids, the declining days of a reign of terror." To do so he had to move from place to place as, one by one, the churches were destroyed.

As he preached, he "sensed the tension they were feeling, not knowing whether the next moment the scream of sirens would scatter them in all directions—which happened not infrequently." On their faces he saw "the torment of doubt and despair, the hunger and thirst for a valid comfort and encouragement that would stand the test." For Thielicke and his congregation, "the Lord's Prayer was able to contain it all. There was not a single question we could not have brought to it and not one that would not have been suddenly transformed if it were put in the form of a prayer."

Thielicke ringingly affirmed that "God is a God of purpose, a God with great fatherly plans for our lives, for the life of his people, and the life of all mankind." He preached that the heavenly Father really does call to us in the dark forest.

A few days after our family moved from Camden, New Jersey, to the Poconos, Johnny and I explored far into the woods and lost our bearings. It was getting dark and we couldn't see the mountain. Tangled in bushes in a swampy area, we jumped from hummock to hummock trying to find a trail, a landmark, a creek.

I was ten, Johnny thirteen. He said we weren't lost at all. I felt very lost. What if we had to stay out all night in the dangerous dark, in a strange woods halfway up a mountain?

Suddenly we saw the road right in front of us, and my anxiety disappeared, melted away in relief. We had found the way home!

Had Johnny and I not stumbled on the road that afternoon—had darkness fallen and found us sitting miserably on mossy hummocks with our feet in the ooze—I know what would have happened. My father, an enormously patient man, would have called out from the house, "Johnny! Harold!" Getting no answer, he would have gotten his flashlight and started walking down the road, calling our names, "Johnny! Harold!"

As soon as we heard his call we would have headed straight for that beloved voice, plunging through the dark forest to meet him, calling out, "Dad! Here we are! We're coming!" With what thankfulness we would have seen the flickers of his flashlight, pinpricks of light bouncing off the black trees and bushes. We would have followed them unswervingly until we could see clearly the wide swath of the hard gravel road.

Aren't we all like children in a forest, searching for the road? The trails we follow inevitably dead-end in tangled underbrush, leaving us deeper in the woods. Dusk turns to dark, and the smoke and grime of life obscure even the stars.

But if we listen in the night, if we stop rustling the dead leaves underfoot and concentrate, eventually we hear our heavenly Father calling out to us. He calls us by name—each one of us. We can miss his voice; the noises of the night distort it. But he keeps calling.

"God constantly encourages us to trust him in the dark," said A. W. Tozer.

When we answer his call, we begin to see his light. It flickers among the thick, dark trees, at times fully revealing those ominous shapes for what they are. We "see through a glass darkly," but we sense that the road leads deeper and deeper and deeper into God's truth, and closer and closer to home.

Some of the surrounding landscape is still not identifiable. Yet glimmers of light appear in unexpected places.

A rabbit screams. A duck grieves. Mysteries. Enigmas. Dark woods. Strange patterns of life and death. A stone homestead long ago buried by bulldozers still taunts my sense of reality. Boyhood friends rush by like a fast-forward videotape.

Jesus said that the very hairs of our heads are numbered and that not a sparrow falls but is seen by the Father. Such a statement sounds naive if not preposterous. Yet scientists believe equally preposterous things.

Some now say the entire universe began in a "big bang" from matter so compressed that at the beginning of the world all the known universe could have been held between your two fingers . . . a truly unthinkable concept. None of us can get our minds around the sizes and distances of galaxies and the phenomena of black holes and quasars. The universe resting between one's fingers! Sheer silliness. Yet the theory conjures up biblical images of creation—of God spreading out his hand and separating the waters.

The main point, however, is that this wild idea is now accepted by many leading scientific thinkers. Is it any more improbable to believe that God the Father has numbered the hairs of our heads or that he sees every sparrow fall . . . or that he cares about each little Ethiopian and Nicaraguan child . . . or that he knows the name of each abused and deserted child in America's cities? Jesus has said it is so.

But even if we do believe that he sees and numbers them, what evidence do we have that he cares . . . that he truly loves the little children? That our prayers for them make any difference?

Scripture tells us we must believe when we pray. "The just shall live by faith," says James. Is this some sort of Catch 22?

No, as we pray, God comes to us like a father and lets us drag all our doubts and fears into his light. When we sense our faith is little, we can ask for more. Like the man who brought his son to Jesus for healing. When he evidenced some doubt about whether Jesus could really help his boy, Jesus told him that anything was possible for those who believe. "I believe!" the father cried. "Help me overcome my unbelief!"

Those of us appalled by the riddle of life pray that same prayer. We cannot untangle the Gordian knot of life and death. Scripture says the "whole creation groans as in travail," waiting for deliverance. Solomon, the wisest of men, complained, "I saw all that God has done. No one can comprehend what goes on under the sun. Despite all his efforts to search it out, man cannot discover its meaning." Like Solomon, we cannot sort it out. But we can pray, "I believe. Help thou mine unbelief."

My pastor, Bob Harvey, tells how early in his ministry a close friend died. In an effort to comfort the widow, also a close friend, Bob shared all his seminary textbook explanations of how and why God might have let this happen. But the woman rebuked him lovingly. "I don't need a God like that," she said. "I don't need to understand all this. What I need is a God who is bigger than my mind."

Dr. Vernon Grounds, former president of Denver Seminary and a compassionate and thoughtful man, wrote this in a recent letter: "One thing which impresses me more and more is the bewildering tragedy of human life. As I counsel with emotionally broken individuals and as I observe the pain, injustice and frustration in the world, I cling tenaciously to my conviction that God, infinitely wise and loving, is sovereign. And the empty tomb demonstrates that out of the worst which can take place, he is able to bring forth his own glorious best. Yet I understand the experience of Caroll E. Simcox who in his 'The Eternal You' confesses that one day he heard God saying, 'I wish you'd leave all this reconciling of things to me, since you are so hopelessly unequipped for it, and that you would use whatever influence you have with your fellow fussers and worriers to do likewise. I know what I'm doing. I'll go over it with you when you get home.' Like Simcox, I have quit worrying and fussing over the intractable problem of evil, confident that God's explanation will completely satisfy my mind and heart."

Such understanding does not come quickly. Vernon Grounds says this after decades as a believer.

We are all familiar with the phrase, "God works in mysterious ways." They are William Cowper's words. Three different times in the past years as our congregation has sung this hymn, I have found myself writing down every word. Cowper, a man who suffered depression and much questioning, came to the same conclusion regarding the depth of God's grace as have Grounds, Simcox, Thielicke, and a host of seasoned believers. His hymn is worth reading slowly and thoughtfully.

God moves in a mysterious way
his wonders to perform;
He plants his footsteps in the sea,
and rides upon the storm.

Deep in unfathomable mines
of never-failing skill,
He treasures up his bright designs,
and works his sovereign will.

Ye fearful saints, fresh courage take;
the clouds ye so much dread
Are big with mercy, and shall break
in blessings on your head.

Judge not the Lord by feeble sense,
but trust him for his grace;
Behind a frowning providence
he hides a smiling face.

His purposes will ripen fast,
unfolding every hour;
The bud may have a bitter taste,
but sweet will be the flower.

Blind unbelief is sure to err,
and scan his work in vain;
God is his own interpreter
and he will make it plain.

Scripture and prayer give us a viewpoint from which we can see God at work in this fecund world of death and life. Only from that vantage point can we see it all through eyes of faith and listen to the children pray:

Now I lay me down to sleep;
I pray the Lord my soul to keep.

Only then can we be comforted with the assurance that though their bodies may not be saved, their souls are eternally safe. We know that Jesus said, "Suffer the little children to come unto me." Our children can come to him today, through prayer—as can we.

Scripture is chillingly realistic about the evil visited upon children. We read of Herod's troops riding into Bethlehem and killing the innocent baby boys, tearing them from their mothers "who could not be comforted." But the Bible's focus in that story is on Jesus, the child of hope whose parents were warned away by angels. The Gospels do not tell us why the angels did not warn the other parents in Bethlehem; they simply point to the light in the darkness.

Scripture is equally frank about the Egyptian Pharaoh who ordered the deaths of all Hebrew baby boys. How many were killed it does not say, but Exodus tells of a mother determined to save her little boy. She hid her baby, Moses, for three months, then put him in an ark and left it in the bullrushes of the Nile. It was an act of desperation. Anyone seeing the child would know he was a Hebrew baby and, presumably, drown him. Surely she prayed fervently as she left the river and went home. Just as surely, she could not have imagined that Pharaoh's daughter would find her son and adopt him, or that she, his own mother, would be asked to wet nurse the child. What an answer to her prayers—an answer she could never have anticipated. But what about the other Hebrew mothers whose babies were not saved?

What is God doing with our children? We believe each child is infinitely precious, made in God's image, but the world does not treat them that way. Still, as we pray, the Father sometimes gives us eyes to see.

A few weeks ago Jeanette and I were at Forest Home in California for a writer's conference. Eight of us were sitting around a breakfast table when someone asked Jeanette if she had children. She showed pictures of Michelle, Todd, and Greg as well as photos of our two foster babies, one of whom has Down's Syndrome.

I was amazed at how those at the table came alive. One woman said softly but with love intense in her eyes, "Yes, I have a special child, too." Her voice and expression told us her handicapped child was special indeed. Another said she had been a foster child herself and still greatly loved her foster mother. A third described how her child had saved her.

"My husband was a gambler," she said, "and he was murdered for his winnings." She began drinking heavily; she would lie around the house, unable to do anything for herself, sliding toward oblivion, helpless to change. "What brought me through was my little child. I didn't want to lose her. I'd do anything for her." Although no other therapy had helped, her love for that child gave her power beyond herself to rise from the depths of alcoholism.

God is at work in and through children. Sometimes we get glimpses of it.

Last summer our church bulletin contained a prayer letter from Karl and Debbie Dortzbach, missionaries in Kenya, in which Debbie told of one of those glimpses she had caught during a visit to a slum in Nairobi.

"The roughly cut door squeaked on rusty hinges as I entered," Debbie wrote. "I saw bare, earthen walls decorated with an old calendar and a few faded black-and-white snapshots of family. The hard-packed, uneven dirt floor had one corner reserved for a charcoal stove and a few cooking utensils." As grim as it was, Debbie said, it was a "cozy refuge from the oozing and rotting garbage" between all the similar "house-rooms" that were homes for forty thousand people. But she was unprepared for what she found in that room: an old woman with a small infant in her arms.

The woman told Debbie that, unable to have children, she had eked out a living in Nairobi selling a few vegetables. "Her prayer—like Hannah of old—had been that God would give her a child. Now she was old, like Sarah, beyond age. But one day, just a few weeks past, she had been returning home when the muffled cries of an infant sent her pushing through the pile of garbage near her house. It was there—cold and abandoned, but alive! Had God answered her prayer? Taking the child first to the police to certify that it was abandoned and not stolen, she asked to keep it. Cleaned and warm, the child slept peacefully in her arms."

The woman had been fearful when Debbie first entered the room. "When I saw a white woman with the health worker, I was afraid that you had come to take the child from me," she said. "But I knew that God would not take back his gift that way."

Debbie summed up her story: "In the midst of despair, Christ offers hope. In poverty, he brings wealth. Right now the rain pelts down on our backs and clings to our shoes, the stench of garbage fills the air. But that muffled cry!—the faint reminder that the Spirit of the living Christ is here."

How can we pray with seeing eyes? By becoming like children ourselves. We have no choice in this. Said Jesus, "Unless you become like children you will never enter the kingdom of God." We must commune with the Father with a sense of childlike wonder.

Even secular thinkers have recognized the importance of a childlike attitude. Psychologist Erik Erikson, in his eighties, spoke of older persons reviving qualities from childhood. "Einstein used the word 'wonder' to describe his experience as a child," Erikson said, "and he was considered childlike by many people. And I think he claimed that he was able to formulate the theory of relativity because he kept asking the questions children ask. So when I say old people think like children, I do not mean childishly, but with wonder, joy, playfulness." And the great artist Picasso said, "It has taken me a whole lifetime to learn to draw like children."

A whole lifetime . . . .

In the same letter in which Vernon Grounds quotes Simcox, he also refers to the prayer of a father in the novel *The Blood of the Lamb* by Peter DeVries. The man's daughter has leukemia and, after several remissions, is finally dying. In his anguish the father goes to a nearby church and prays that she may be spared for just one year longer. In his prayer he shares his daughter's sense of wonder, and he promises what they will do with that "one more year."

"We will spend it as we have the last, missing nothing. We will mark the dance of every hour between the snowdrop and the snow: crocus to tulip to violet to iris to rose. We will note not only the azalea's crimson flowers but the red halo that encircles awhile the azalea's root when her petals are shed; also the white halo that rings for a week the foot of the old catalpa tree. Later we will prize the chrysanthemums which last so long, almost as long as paper flowers, perhaps because they know in blooming not to bloom. We will seek out the leaves turning in the little-praised bushes and the unadvertized trees. Everyone loves the sweet, neat blossom of the hawthorn in spring, but who lingers over the olive drab of her leaf in autumn? We will. We will note the lost yellows in the tangles of that bush that spills over the Howard's stone wall, the meek hues among which it seems to hesitate before comitting itself to red, and next year learn its name. We will seek out these modest subtleties so lost in the blare of the oaks and maples, like flutes and wood-winds drowned in brasses and drums. When winter comes, we will let no snow fall ignored. We will again watch the first blizzard from her window like figures locked snug in a glass paperweight. 'Pick one out and follow it to the ground!' she will say again. We will feed the plain birds that stay to cheer us through the winter, and when spring returns we shall be the first out, to catch the snowdrop's first white whisper in the wood. All this we ask, with the remission of our sins, in Christ's name. Amen."

A sense of childlike wonder at what God is doing on earth.

A prayer to see, at least a little, as God sees.

7
LIVING BY MYSTERY

Yesterday maybe I saw this crazy turning of the terrible on its head, this breaking through the worst with the breath of grace.

The car battery was dead so I decided to hike the seven miles to East Stroudsburg University from which I graduated twenty-five years ago. My sister-in-law, Donna, works there and would drive me home after I did some shopping.

I hiked down miles of trails, then onto the highway. After two hours of brisk walking, I reached the campus. The wind was cold; I was glad to duck into the building where Donna worked.

She was in the hall and introduced me to a colleague named Marcia. It turned out Marcia and I had a mutual friend who had shown remarkable courage after contracting polio. Then Marcia and Donna mentioned a woman, widowed twice, who had also accepted her lot bravely.

"Sometimes in the worst of circumstances," I commented, "we see God at work."

"Oh," Marcia said immediately, "we've certainly seen that!" And she told me how at twenty-one her son's wife Dinah—bright, energetic, well-liked—had suffered a stroke. As she was recovering, Marcia sat by her and asked if she was afraid. Dinah nodded yes. Marcia repeated the doctor's assurance that she should be able to overcome the stroke's effects. "I then went to get her sister," Marcia said, "and when I re-entered the room, Dinah was having a massive cerebral hemorrhage."

Dinah was in a coma six weeks. "The doctors gave us no hope. There were no brain signs. One doctor even asked in exasperation, 'What are we fighting for here anyway?'"

I remembered that Donna had called Jeanette about Dinah, requesting that we pray for her, and our prayer group had done so. Apparently people all over the country had prayed for her.

"Today, Dinah really is a happy person," Marcia said, as if she could hardly believe it herself. Against all expectations, Dinah finally did come out of the coma, but, she was paralyzed and unable to speak coherently. Eventually, however, they were able to communicate with her and asked about the six weeks she had been in the coma. Had she been aware of them around her bed, wanting her back? Yes, definitely. Dinah then indicated she had somehow seen her mother, who had died when she was twelve, and she had sensed God's presence.

"Did God tell you to come back?" they asked her.

"No."

"Did your mother tell you to come back?"

"Yes."

Previous to the coma, Dinah had always been very sad about losing her mother. "But she's never been sad about that since," Marcia said. "Dinah and Doug are both happy people. My son Doug says, 'Our life is just different, that's all.' At first for Dinah to get a shower might take a half a day, but he didn't complain. Now she's progressed to riding her electric wheelchair to the store. Doug calls ahead so they can help her in."

Marcia went on to tell us of little joys and triumphs they were experiencing, and even humor. She said it again of this young couple, as if still hardly believing it herself: "They're really happy people."

Out of the worst, God brings wonder. That hallway conversation stays with me long after I've returned to the house, uplifting my spirits. I have the sense that "God is up to something."

Questions nag, of course. How long will this young couple stay happy? And if all those prayers could bring her back, why couldn't they get her completely healed? But stronger than the questions was my realization that something connected with other dimensions was going on.

Mysteries. Was it just possible the Lord had blessed that battery dead?

I sit at the kitchen table, books, papers, and writing pads stacked all over it, coffee cup in hand. I pick up Bob Benson's book, *He Speaks Softly.* Bob died soon after the book was published, less than a year ago; he was not much older than I.

Reading his book is like listening to an old friend spin yarns. I remember Bob about fifteen years ago when we worked together on a project. Handsome, thoughtful, a book and music publisher, he was easygoing and unaffected. He wrote several warm and insightful books about his family. The title of one, *Laughter in the Walls,* typified the joyous way he had of drawing meaning out of everyday life.

Then Bob got cancer. He battled it for years, and at

one point all hope was gone. He speaks only obliquely in his book about a special touch from God bringing him back. There are no descriptions of his illness in this unpretentious but wonderfully wise book, only homespun tales about the ways God works in our lives.

I'm fascinated by the deep insights in Bob's stories of people finding the good in tragic circumstances. At one point he tells of asking people in retreat prayer times to remember good events from their pasts, and then to write them down. As they did so, he would watch their faces reflect peace and pleasure. After that, he asked them to list the bad events—the dark times that threatened to engulf their souls—and would watch their expressions change to pain. He would then close by emphasizing that God is the Lord of both lists.

Time after time, Bob said, people would come up to him afterward and tell him they didn't know in which category to place certain experiences. "Some of those things are so evil," they would tell him, "it would seem their place would be a foregone conclusion. The day they happened I knew, all right. The bottom of the bottom wasn't low enough. . . . I thought I was going to die. But now, looking back, I'm not so sure." Bob saw in their eyes depths that showed "both joy and sorrow, both peace and pain."

Hope and realism mixed together shine through the words of this man so close to death himself at the time. He saw that even our most dreaded experiences may contain God's best surprises.

Our connection with Mel and Jane Sorenson began in the sixties when Jeanette, a registered nurse, cared for Jane at Central DuPage Hospital as she recovered from cancer surgery. My next recollection is of seeing them not long afterward at a morning worship service with their daughter Linda, an attractive blonde teenager. I whispered to Jeanette that I had never seen their daughter before, and she explained that Linda was on a visit from an institution.

Until she was around twelve, Linda had been a normal child, but then she began showing symptoms of schizophrenia. All their prayers and the help of doctors and psychiatrists could not stop the long slide into the institution. Later, as I got to know Jane and Mel and thought of my own blonde little girl, I realized how terrible it must have been to have Linda normal all those years and then, in a pattern common to the affliction, change at puberty.

One Sunday during the time I faced the lawsuit pressures at CTi, Jane and I stood talking in the crowded narthex of our church. Her right arm was still about twice its normal size as a result of her cancer surgery. Mel had gone through a series of tough job reversals, and Linda had experienced many sad difficulties in the state institution. Yet as a faithful part of our prayer group, they always showed as much concern for others as for their own problems.

Jane asked about the lawsuit. I told her that our prayers had been answered, not just in the court process but in the powerful effect the entire experience had had on our staff. We then talked about the moving of God's grace in the lives of several people in the prayer group.

"How wonderful," Jane said, "to be part of a church where there are so many people growing!" She said it with joy, and as soon as she said it, the same thought struck us both; what an ironic statement, considering all the pain in the church.

Some members were grieving for children who had died; others, who had themselves been abused as children, now found their inner chaos tearing them and their families apart; still others felt betrayed by close friends. Jane voiced our mutual thoughts quietly: "It's because there is so much suffering here, isn't it?"

We went on to discuss our total dependence on God. "Twenty years ago," she said, "I couldn't identify with that verse, 'Without Christ I can do nothing.' I could do lots of things, and do them well. But now I know it's true."

It had taken Jane a long time to accept the fact that Linda must remain in an institution, but after she did, her prayer was, "Lord, if you can't fully heal her, then please, at least keep her safe." However, not long after our conversation in the narthex she and Mel had another deep, deep valley to walk. A male patient entered Linda's room and attacked her, stabbing her dozens of times in the head and body. When medical personnel rushed her to an emergency room, they thought it an empty gesture.

Yet Linda's body clung to life. The brutal stabbing had left her blinded and totally paralyzed. Mel and Jane wondered, as we all prayed together at church, if it would be best if Linda went to be with her heavenly Father.

But Linda lived. She gained limited use of one arm and eventually enough sight in one eye to do a little reading. She was now deeply fearful, however, and she needed special medical care for her multiple problems that most hospitals are unable to give. Mel and Jane would take her to hospitals that then would decide they couldn't keep her. It was another traumatic time for them.

Through all this, the Sorensons sensed glimmers of God's grace bleeding through. Though many of their prayers seemed to have been thrown back into their faces, they still kept faith and continued to pray and intercede for others. We sensed in them the remarkable grace that could only have been shaped by adversity.

God at work, even in the worst of events.

As I sit with my pad and books, over the radio comes the hymn, "When peace like a river attendeth my way. . . ." The music swells in a magnificent finale, "It is well! It is well with my soul!" I recall reading that the composer wrote that song after all four of his children had been killed in a shipwreck.

Many of our greatest hymns were composed out of pain. Joseph Scriven's first fiancée drowned the evening they were to be married. His second fiancée died of pneumonia. Scriven never did marry, but out of these tragic events came his remarkable song, "What a Friend We Have in Jesus."

Pain is often the dark through which the light shines. The sun is at its most dramatic bursting through black clouds.

A few months ago I sat across the table from a man who, in the course of our meal, was asked a tough question. For years this man had been attacked professionally and had experienced painful family problems. Yet year after year he graciously and effectively carried his responsibilities. His answer to the tough question that day showed his usual depth and grace. A man sitting next to me leaned over and remarked, "I used to hate what was happening to him. But now I see it took all he went through to enable him to answer like that."

Another man, a friend who has worked hard for Christian causes, found out not long ago that his wife had been having an affair. He was dumbfounded; he was furious; he raged against his wife and her lover. He made all sorts of threats and felt his marriage had been ripped apart forever. But over the course of time, with the help of his church and much prayer, he forgave his wife and they began rebuilding their marriage. His friends began to notice quantum leaps in the depth of his spiritual life, compassion, and godly insights.

It reminds me of the old proverb: "Blessings and curses are opposite ends of the same stick."

God at work in the worst of events. I am sitting at the table looking at the bowling-pin lamp Richie made as a schoolboy. It reminds me of the phone call more than fifteen years ago when my mother told me that Mrs. Prosser had been murdered. "The police want to talk to Richie," she said. And we knew it was likely he had done it.

After my mother's call I stepped out of the house and started walking, bewildered and angry. After all our efforts and prayers, how could it have turned out this way? I seethed inside, trying to sort it out but not succeeding.

I walked along a stretch of the Illinois Prairie Path, an old railroad right of way banked above fields and creeks. I moved briskly, my body working pleasurably and effectively, but my mind in turmoil. Finally, I burst out to God, "How could you do this! Just when Richie was responding, he was pulled out of our home. Of course he slid into trouble! And Mrs. Prosser—who just lost her husband and best friend—is murdered!" I talked to the Lord that way for a long time, letting all my emotions flare.

When I noticed a dried-up pond ringed by cattails, I stopped. A few weeks earlier I had noticed it full of thick algae and dying fish; now it was merely cracked mud.

When the pond was dying, dozens of little fish stuck their mouths and gills into the air, desperate either for air or escape from that stagnant water. "Weren't they just like Richie?" I demanded of the Lord. "Just like us? It's not only Richie—it's all the people caught like him, all the victims who go on to victimize. How can you run your world with such brutality?" I asked, tears in my eyes.

Never before had I prayed quite like that; and the response was crystal clear: "I'm not upset by your prayers." On the contrary, it was as if he had been waiting for me to look evil full in the face and confront him. "I've been waiting for you to talk to me like this. Don't you think this has caused me anguish, too? How do you think I feel about Richie? And all the others like him? And Mrs. Prosser? Haven't I wept over them? Haven't I sent my only Son to die for them?"

All this flowed into me with the force not of "answers" but of powerful connections with God—personal, actual, with a sense of purpose and peace in their wake. I sensed the Lord was drawing me into his perspective, that he was calling me almost as a colleague to join forces in extending his love, to intercede for others in their helplessness . . . and that he was indeed in charge, transcending the tragedies.

Since that experience, I have often been intrigued by such outbursts in the Scriptures. The psalmists and the prophets include many passages like my anguished Prairie Path prayer. When Job, with good reason, asked God such questions, the response was simply a magnificent description of God's power.

Habakkuk, though, is the one I identify with most of all. He asked God the same maddening riddles that have plagued men and women for millennia. His three-chapter book near the end of the Old Testament is thoroughly modern. He saw people corrupted, cheated, and falsely imprisoned—and he prayed earnestly about it. Yet nothing changed. In exasperation he cried out, "How long, O Lord, must I call for help, but you do not listen?" He complained to God, "The law is paralyzed, and justice never prevails. The wicked hem in the righteous, so that justice is perverted." Not much different from our world. Even in our democracy with its justice through law, we find scandal and a downward spiral of despair.

After Habakkuk had expressed his indignation, he got his answer—and it wasn't at all what he expected or wanted. God told him to look around at the other nations and to be astounded. The Lord was going to clean house by bringing the Babylonians against Habakkuk's people. God described these foreigners as ruthless, fierce, bent on violence, "guilty men, whose own strength is their god."

Habakkuk was astounded all right, astounded and incensed. He practically sputtered back at God, asking him how he could possibly appoint the Babylonians—of all people!—to execute judgment on Judah. How could God use the wicked to swallow up people more righteous than they? The Babylonians were barbarians, Habakkuk pointed out, far more cruel and violent and godless than his own nation.

How readily I identify with Habakkuk. While my prayers are often of intercession and praise, they are just as often intense wrestling with God over his seemingly inexplicable ways.

Did Habakkuk get a direct answer? Not at all. God simply said the Babylonians were coming—he could count on it. And then God made the statement upon which Martin Luther founded the Reformation: "The just shall live by faith."

In a sense, that's all Habakkuk was given to hold onto. God told him the Babylonians would get theirs, too, and that their judgment would be sure. Then God completed his response with that statement so often sung in our worship services: "The Lord is in his holy temple; let all the earth be silent before him."

One might think Habakkuk would slouch off in despair. But—and I find this most amazing of all—he did just the opposite. He prayed, "Lord, I have heard of your fame; I stand in awe of your deeds, O Lord. Renew them in our day, in our time make them known; in wrath remember mercy." Then he talked about God's glory covering the heavens and his praise the earth. "His splendor was like the sunrise; rays flashed from his hand." He described the incredible power of God who "splits the earth" and makes "mountains writhe." Then Habakkuk predicted an end of evil:

In wrath you strode through the earth
and in anger you threshed the nations.
You came out to deliver your people,
to save your anointed one.
You crushed the leader of the land of wickedness,
you stripped him from head to foot.
With his own spear you pierced his head. . . .

God communicated his full majesty and power to Habakkuk, emphasizing that somehow, in his own way, he would bring about righteousness and justice. Habakkuk's heart pounded and his lips quivered and his legs trembled at all this; yet he managed a remarkable statement of faith.

"I will wait patiently for the day of calamity to come on the nation invading us. Though the fig tree does not bud and there are no grapes on the vines, though the olive crop fails and the fields produce no food, though there are no sheep in the pen and no cattle in the stalls, yet I will rejoice in the Lord, I will be joyful in God my Savior."

Quite a statement. Total trust. And if we are to have faith in God's ultimate victory over evil, it will have to be much the same. Evil is pervasive; suffering is endemic. Yet, as Habakkuk learned, despite confusing and disillusioning and even deadly circumstances, we can be filled with praise.

"The Sovereign Lord is my strength," Habakkuk says at the end of his little book. "He makes my feet like the feet of a deer, he enables me to go on the heights."

8
LIVING BY INTERCESSION

The old blacktop road I am walking is steep and difficult. Thousands of times before I sped up this mountain in a school bus or car, but now I hesitate as I think of climbing on foot the long curves to the top. When I hear the sound of the creek far off in the laurel, I leave the road and head toward it.

The creek is full of November rains, rushing over boulders and exposed tree roots. I try to walk by the water, but the laurel and brush are too thick. Oh, for a path! Crawling through the underbrush along the creek would take forever. But the other choice is the steep road.

I hesitate for a moment and almost turn away. Then, grimacing, I plunge into the laurel, pushing, twisting, shoving. This could go on forever, I think, bending under a thick, low branch and then stretching out to pull myself through. I finally squirm past the laurel to an open stretch along the creek and walk on the pine needles at water's edge.

Then I see it. Something I never would have guessed was here. I actually say aloud, "This I cannot believe," as I stare at the wide-open space before me. A few hundred feet away is a beautiful waterfall. Beautiful not only because of its height but because of the crashing water upstream from it, the parklike expanse of pine surrounding it, and the banks rising steeply a hundred feet above me, thick with laurel and pine, making it a secluded, enchanted glade. "This can't be here," I think. I stand in one spot for at least five minutes, stunned by the beauty surpassing anything I've seen so far on my hikes, stunned by having been completely unaware that all this existed here in very familiar territory.

I explore the open glade and find an old campfire close to the mist from the falls. I climb to the top of the steep embankment and see a series of flat massifs over which the water sluices in sheets. On a higher ridge I find a path leading to a deep pool split out of the rock like a giant hot tub under the pine needles. As I explore, I cannot stop shaking my head in wonder. All this has been here all the time, right under my nose. I passed it on the school bus every day and on every trip to town.

Across the creek I come upon the Appalachian Trail. As I begin climbing it, into my mind like rushing water flow parallels to prayer—that it is much like stepping into that glade. The similarities intrigue me. Crashing through those laurel took effort. I had to force my way past the leafy, green barrier, but once past it, I stepped into the unexpected beauty of that waterfall.

It was like so many of my prayer experiences. The wonders of connecting with God are right there by the side of the road. The sound of the water is inviting, yet all kinds of thickets discourage us. It takes so much trouble to get started. And isn't the fast highway of "getting things done" more important? Yet when we do crash through those thickets, we find—not every time, but surprisingly often—the unexpected joy.

That happens especially with intercessory prayer.

Intercessory prayer. That term is hardly user-friendly. For most people it conjures up either guilt or a yawn. It's one of those terms that once held explosive meaning for saints burning with holy passion. Now it seems obsolete, outmoded, something to be read about in religious classics but no longer relevant.

Intercessory prayer. I remember wondering years ago if that weren't the work of those old lady "prayer warriors" who couldn't do anything else as they rocked away the years. Or was it something men in monasteries did, men who had nothing else to do all day?

Intercessory prayer. To most it's an infelicitous phrase, masking a virile reality—as if the Pittsburgh Steelers were named the Iron City Daffodils.

Yet Scripture's references to intercession are so powerful it's easy to see why our forebears were so enthused about it. I can still remember sitting in a Wednesday night prayer meeting as a teenager, staring at and absorbing the remarkable statement, "The Holy Spirit itself maketh intercession for us with groanings which cannot be uttered." What a dramatic concept: the Holy Spirit prays for us with an intensity beyond expression. Intercession invokes such passion in the Holy Spirit that words cannot describe it. And he is praying that way for us! God himself, third person of the Trinity, prays for us with total empathy, with, to recall Thielicke's image, a "scorched hand" as he reaches down to us in love. Here is Scripture's image of God, filled with longing, agonizing in prayer for you and me. This remarkable drama goes on all the time, yet we're generally as oblivious to it as I was to that waterfall, passing it unknowingly year after year.

Of course, the idea of God in passionate prayer for us

should not be new. Jesus, after he had exposed himself to the flames of evil and hatred, enduring the cross and humiliation here on earth, continued praying for us, as he is doing right now. The resurrected Jesus, Scripture tells us, "ever lives to make intercession for us."

Arrows through the windows of our minds!

Wouldn't Jesus rather be doing something more interesting, like creating exotic planets? Is it really possible that he's so concerned about us that he "lives to intercede for us"?

If God the Holy Spirit and God the Son are both right now praying fervently for us, shouldn't this give us a clue about how we might set our own priorities? It might also give us a clue about the only possible means to obey him. He told us that if we love him, we are to obey his commands. Jesus also kept emphasizing he could do nothing without the Father, and he spent whole nights in prayer.

At that meeting at Forest Home last month, Jeanette and I sat in the little glass chapel listening to Sherwood Wirt, editor emeritus of *Decision* magazine, tell of a bruising set of events years before that had wounded him deeply, tempting him toward feelings of bitterness. At that time he attended meetings of the Canadian Revival, "the only genuine revival I was ever involved with." He was touched by it, and as a result Woody invited a Canadian couple who were part of the revival to hold special meetings in Minneapolis where he lived.

During the course of this couple's ministry in that city, they laid their hands on Woody's head and prayed for him.

Woody felt nothing except a little foolish kneeling there, he said. In fact, he had agreed to it somewhat reluctantly. But they told him the Holy Spirit would work in him. Woody wondered about it, but a few days later, "I felt as though I had fallen into a vat of love," he told us as we sat in the chapel. "Ever since that time, I have never felt bitter toward anyone."

Woody went on to show from the Scriptures, convincingly, that love is the primary mark of the Holy Spirit in a life. Only six weeks before, Woody had lost his beloved wife, Winnie, to cancer. Yet he was there ministering to us. After the meeting, I said to a writer who lived near Woody, "I remember when he came back from that revival and how beautiful his spirit was as he told us of it. He really showed that love."

She replied, "We who have been with him this past year see how real it still is. He lives it!"

Even as I write this, I wish I could hug Woody as I pray for him from Pennsylvania. Love. The primary mark of the Holy Spirit.

What Woody experienced dovetails perfectly with Jesus' own emphasis to his disciples just before the soldiers took him. He told them that whoever obeyed his commands loved him and was loved by the Father. But Jesus didn't say what his commands were. Instead, he talked about vines and branches; he said he was the vine and his disciples the branches. If I had been an early disciple, I would have been wondering about then what commands might make me or break me in Jesus' eyes. Finally Jesus came right out with it. "My command is this: love each other as I have loved you."

And just before he said that, he told them, "I have told you this so that my joy may be in you and that your joy may be complete."

Love others. Jesus commands it. It's the way to joy, he says.

There's only one catch. How can we love others if we feel jaded or rejected or betrayed? How can we love others when we would rather set them straight? Or let them know how much they've hurt us? When we're bitter or frustrated and have good cause to be, we simply cannot conjure up love. To make the picture worse, Jesus said "love each other as I have loved you." Thoroughly impossible!

Such love comes only from God and is the natural consequence of prayer.

One of the ways we learn to love others is by interceding for them—by praying for them as Jesus did and thereby seeing them through God's eyes. As Jesus is "ever praying" for us, as the Holy Spirit prays with groans that cannot be uttered, we join them, and through the hard work and duty of prayer for others begin to experience both joy and love for them.

A beautiful illustration of this principle at work is told by Bishop John V. Taylor in the story of a Russian artisan who began praying for a peasant named Nicholas. "In the beginning, I prayed with tears of compassion for Nicholas, his young wife, for the little child. But as I was praying, the sense of the divine presence began to grow on me, and at a certain moment it grew so powerful, that I lost sight of Nicholas, his wife, his child, his needs, their village, and I could be aware only of God; and I was drawn by the sense of a divine presence, deeper and deeper, until at a sudden at the heart of this presence, I met the divine love holding Nicholas, his wife, and his child; and now it was with the love of God that I began to pray for them again. But again I was drawn into the deep, and into the depths of this, I again found the divine love."

Intercessory prayer, joining with God at his work, becomes at times a unique experience of grace. It can also be a process through which God speaks to us and instructs us. My favorite example of this is an incident from the life of John "Praying" Hyde, missionary to India.

Hyde was praying for a pastor, pouring out his heart:

"'O God! Thou knowest that brother how . . . '—'cold' he was going to say, when suddenly a Hand seemed to be laid on his lips, and a Voice said to him in stern reproach, 'He that toucheth him, toucheth the apple of Mine eye.'"

John Hyde was horrified. He felt guilty of accusing his brother and confessed his own sin of self-righteousness. He thought of the verse, "Whatsoever things are lovely . . . if there be any virtue, if there be any praise, think on these things." He cried out to the Lord to show him those things in this man's life that were lovely and of good report. He thought of the man's hard work, of his tact and his ability to heal quarrels, and of his being a fine husband. He was reminded of one fine quality after another, so he spent all the rest of his prayer time in praise for this man.

What also rings true for me in the story is that when Hyde next had contact with this pastor, he learned that the man had received "a great spiritual uplift."

One of the benefits of intercessory prayer is the way it changes us!

When his own efforts at loving this brother had failed, John Hyde was able to obey Jesus' primary command to love through prayer. Once Hyde was on his knees in intercession, God not only was able to rebuke Hyde's feelings of superiority, but was able to pour godly love into his heart.

How can we get off the dull, blacktop roads of inertia and into the refreshing glades of intercessory prayer? Crashing through laurel thickets seldom seems convenient when we can zip up a smooth road on four wheels, and we're under a lot of pressure to get there fast.

As I walk these woods day by day, a second analogy runs through my mind. I think of traditional descriptions of fairies at night out in the forest, reveling and sparkling with delight. Humans, they say, can stalk quietly through the dark woods in search of the happy sprites and suddenly come upon the flickering revelry. But the instant a fairy spots a human—poof, they disappear.

Jesus came that "our joy may be full." All over the woods we're in—this terrible dark-night woods of cancer and murder and betrayal—from the fringes of the forest we hear distant sounds of parties and joymaking. People like Wirt and Hyde get filled with power and peace, and remarkable things happen. Flickering in the darkness out there, we sense something real. Will it elude us? We stalk the night, searching for reality, and we come upon the celebrants dancing in light radiating from the depths of their souls. And what happens?

Good news! Unlike the fairies and wood sprites, this reality doesn't flit away! We're invited to the party! It's God's party and we have goldleaf invitations. We just have to crash through enough laurel and stalk the sounds of merrymaking so we can find and join the celebrants.

Not that all prayer is a celestial romp. Sometimes it seems all we do is crash through laurel. Sometimes we can't hear the sounds of merrymaking at all. But like Habakkuk, we combine aggressive prayer with patient waiting for God, knowing that at least now and then—and ultimately forever—we will rejoice and be "exceeding glad."

As Habakkuk put it:

I will rejoice in the Lord.
I will joy in the God of my salvation.
The Lord God is my strength;

He will make my feet like deer's feet,
And He will make me walk on my high hills.

An entry from my prayer journal says:

It's nonsense that intercession is a terrible obligation. I just sat down going over names and putting a mark by each one, asking God to bless, and then adding some more names. What washed over me was an enormous gratitude for all the wonderful friends I have, all the people I can pray for. Starting, and sometimes plodding through, can be tedious—but it puts me in a loving framework with those I care about and long for, even those miles away. Prayer becomes the most thrilling time of the day; it puts me at one with people around me. Obviously, I must pray not just for friends, but also for "enemies." When I pray for them, it's hard to be all churned up inside about "what they are doing to me."

At another point I wrote:

Just finished praying for a long list of people. The benefits:

** The joy of knowing you've been at God's work, laboring with him for souls, the most valuable of all.*

** The promise the prayers will be heard and will move God's hand of blessing.*

** Its effect on my attitudes. A niece I have been neglecting—next time I'm with her, I'll work more at showing her love.*

** Somehow the dark weight of frustrations about the man who can obstruct my plans ebbs at least partially away.*

** The anxiety I feel for ____________, who is fouling up his life far away where I can do nothing, is changed to a peace that he is in God's hands and God will act.*

These names—sixty-seven of them—did it really take all that much time to remember them and ask God to move into their lives? Only ten or fifteen minutes, and now my emotions toward all these people at this moment is one of love and caring. Prayer changes their lives, but it moves in me, too, and changes all my perspective for the day.

Part of me hesitates to share these entries from my personal journal. I don't want to suggest any legalistic system of how many people to pray for or how to pray for them. Sometimes I pray for many in brief prayers; at other times I pray earnestly and long for a few. I've experimented with all sorts of systems and non-systems and lay no approach on anyone, nor do I claim to be consistently faithful myself. Systems break down and fail. I fail.

My latest attempt at a system for intercessory prayer is to use Thank You cards. Inside each I write names—family, colleagues, friends, "enemies." The bold Thank You in the front then reminds me of the enormous privilege of connecting with these unique persons, each an awesome human being made in God's image.

The fruit of the Spirit is love, joy . . . ; these two are intertwined. The fruit of the Spirit chapter, Galatians 5, ends with "Let's not provoke and envy each other." Provoking and envying are natural to us, but they can be transformed.

As we visit each person in prayer, we visit holy ground. We begin to see each person as God does. "Oh, how he loves us!" Then it is our privilege to share God's love and envision those persons bathed in God's light. Thereafter, when we meet them, work with them, get into great conflicts with them, we begin to sense that God's love truly can transform them, as surely we cannot.

The other caution is that many times prayer is the desert part of the adventure. Sometimes we just plod through names in prayer and feel as we did when we began. There is not always a waterfall. Sometimes it feels like you're crashing through laurel the whole time and just can't find the path. But you keep at it, noting, as I also wrote in my journal: *Prayer is hard work.*

Yet I won't take back a bit about the fairies at midnight or the waterfall-surprise.

9
LIVING BY BLESSEDNESS

Past midnight. Before going to bed, I flick on the outside lights. Transformation! Snow covers everything. Maple and pine branches bend with its weight. As I look to the outer edge of the light, my eyes bug. A giant white tarantula, ten feet across and three feet high, is advancing on the house! The impression lasts a full second, until I realize it's a gooseberry bush, branches thick with snow and bowed out like a spider's legs.

Surprises real and imagined.

In the morning, after breakfast, I step outside. The snow is so heavy it has broken willow branches. I drag some off the driveway.

No tire tracks disturb the road—just virgin snow and deer and rabbit tracks. Everything's white. Birches hang into the road. I shake a few loose, but they rise only partway. A motorist, to make progress, would have to get out every hundred yards and shake trees.

Hello! What's this? The normally black spaghetti-thin telephone wires have become three-inch-thick white cables, draped in parallel strands like nouveau-art bridge cables. Behind them, hardwoods and evergreens, white with snow, reach out to a brilliant blue sky, like a color tranparency with light behind it. A pale, leftover moon floats like a wispy cloud. A cardinal flies into the woods, bright-red against the white. In a tall hickory are dried grapes, each cluster with a little cap of snow.

I walk the road, shaking birches to release them into the air, staring again and again at the brilliant blue of the sky framing majestic oak, hickory, poplar, and cedar. I stand transfixed at the white wonder and say softly, "Lord, teach me to pray."

And instantly comes a response. "I am. Look at all this!"

"Yes," I whisper, "yes."

Celebrate the temporary! This moment! I struggle not to allow thoughts of human turmoil to mar it.

A hawk flaps out of a spruce and cruises off toward the mountain. I notice a telephone line thick with snow still connects to a corner of my grandfather's house, though no one has lived there for thirty years. I wonder what forest creatures now call it home.

Spruce trees by the old spring hang into deep snow like tall, bent dolls. I shake them vigorously, and they spring up a few feet. I could go around for hours shaking trees free. Like people you try to help, they don't spring erect. The birches and spruce just lift partway as if the weight has permanently bent their trunks, as if they will never again stand tall like that unbowed, shagbark hickory next to them. Yet I walk around and shake them anyway, lightening their loads, hoping they'll regain their height.

At the top of the big willow, the sun streams through

the broken branches. The ice glitters, frozen traceries of sunlight like Belgian lace.

"Lord, thank you," I say. "Thanks for eyes to see."

Inside, I make a Lebanon bologna sandwich and hot tea for lunch. I glance out the window and am startled by what seems totally improbable and full of grace: the snow on all three wires—thick, white cables above the road—disconnects simultaneously and falls perfectly parallel into the snow. Blessed Trinity. Harmony. Symbolism everywhere.

As I eat and make notes about my morning walk, the scenes remind me of white Christmases past. I remember as a teenager finding a tree in the woods, shaking off the snow, chopping it down, and hauling it home along with a pile of branches. We hung the branches over the doorways and strung our Christmas cards below them. In Norwegian custom, our family opened presents on Christmas Eve, preceded by anchovies and hard-boiled eggs on crispbread, Nicholost and Gjetost cheese. A blessed time.

But many do not have white and blessed Christmases. For them it is just another time of pain, poverty, and loss, made more poignantly so by contrast. As others gather around brightly lighted trees, counting blessings on long, long lists, they see only sorrow.

The first psalm calls the person who loves God's word "blessed"; he or she is like a tree planted by a river, contrasted with the ungodly chaff the wind blows away. But as Ecclesiastes tells us, sometimes the godly person gets paid off like the wicked, and sometimes vice versa.

Who is blessed? Some who pray fervently, who believe and love and serve, feel as if they are the ones blown away like chaff. Can they be called blessed?

A few years ago, just after Christmas, a mother of four young children sat weeping at our kitchen table in

Illinois. Her husband had told her he would stay with her only through Christmas. That afternoon he had left.

A member of our prayer group, Karen was dark-haired and attractive; normally she was quite slender, but now her features were even more angular—she had lost twenty pounds that month. She looked up from her quiet weeping, her face gaunt with grief, and said, "At the church Christmas pageant this year, I was thinking something different from the rest." As I looked across the table at Karen, the mention of the pageant brought to mind the lovely manger scene in our sanctuary and all the little children bringing gifts to the Christ child. Karen's children had walked with the others to the manger to give something to Baby Jesus.

Karen talked very slowly. "The angel said to Jesus, 'Blessed are you among women.' Yet Mary was to carry an illegitimate child. She was to flee with her baby for their lives. She was to see her son crucified. And I thought at the Christmas pageant, 'Am I, too, blessed among women?'"

Like Mary, Karen was bearing stigma and pain. All her fervent prayers for her marriage seemed to have fallen like stones into the sea. What sort of future could be called "blessed" with no money, no husband, no father for her children?

She quoted Mary's words, "Be it unto thy handmaid." Instead of the warm, fuzzy Christmas thoughts most of us were having at that pageant, Karen's had been of the illegitimacy, flight, and crucifixion that lay ahead of that mother and baby.

Was Karen blessed among women? Was Mary?

The angel Gabriel announced that she was: "Blessed are you among women. The Lord is with you!"

"Am I, too, blessed among women?" Karen's question is universal. How many women today are in her situation, looking to God's promises, wondering how ignominy and pain can mean blessedness?

Mary accepted God's surprises, whatever the implications. Gabriel's announcement to this young girl was not only breathtaking and inconceivable but also frightening: "Blessed are you among women." The greeting troubled her, and Gabriel had to reassure her, "Don't be afraid." She had found favor with God. And then the incredible announcement—that she would bear Jesus, Son of the Most High, who would reign forever.

Mary, a virgin, responded, "It's impossible." But Gabriel told her it would be an act of the Holy Spirit. Mary's faith and prayerful attitude enabled her to accept this strange prediction, this surprise beyond all surprises. We are so familiar with the Christmas story that we forget how stunning this must have been to Mary, how the announcement brought as much heartache as joy. Later in the temple, Simeon would tell Mary, "A sword shall pierce your own soul, also." But for now all of Gabriel's words to Mary were of celebration and good news. "With God nothing will be impossible."

I smile as I sit here eating my Gjetost and bread, thinking of a past Christmas party when someone said humorously: "Hark! The Harold Angels." What if God had given me, Harold, the angel Gabriel's job? What would I have said to Mary? Being melancholic by nature, I probably would have added at least a touch of realism, of what lay ahead. But Gabriel said nothing of this. He declared with unmitigated joy that Mary had found favor with God and that her son Jesus would be great and be called Son of the Highest and that the Holy Spirit would come upon her and the power of the Highest overshadow her.

It was the same when the angel of the Lord appeared to Zechariah, announcing the birth of his son, John. The angel did not say John the Baptist would eat insects, go around half-naked, denounce his father's fellow priests, and finally get himself beheaded. No, the angel announced, "Your prayer is heard and you'll have joy and gladness and many will rejoice at his birth."

"Great things happen to those who pray . . . ." The angel told Zechariah his prayers had been answered; he told Mary she'd found favor with God. Great things did happen to these two, and the second half of that statement—"and we learn to pray best in suffering"—seems irrelevant when we think of Christmas joys, of shepherds and wise men and a baby in swaddling clothes. Yet it is not irrelevant, for Zechariah and Mary lived in the brutal Roman world. Certainly God knew this, and what awaited them in the future. But the focus of his messenger angel was not on the evil, but on what God was doing. "Zechariah, your prayers have been heard! Mary, you have found favor with God!"

We're told such "great things" are happening right now, all around us, as we pray. They are happening in Karen's life, and in mine, and in Jeanette's. Only God and the angels see most of it, but our prayers are heard!

Often it does not seem so. Zechariah probably wondered for years if his prayers were futile; and Elizabeth had prayed decade after decade with no answer. When the answer finally did come, he wasn't able to believe it. And what did Mary think some thirty years later when Gabriel's glorious promises seemed mocked by her son's humiliation and execution? Yet in every event, Mary's understanding and faith deepened . . . and then came the unimagined surprise and joy of the resurrection.

Was Mary blessed of God? Yes. Gloriously, painfully, in perplexity and faith, in forebodings and blessings, in watching her son being crucified, in rejoicing at his resurrection, and in being separated from him again. Mary was blessed.

Is Karen blessed of God? Yes, today she would say so. Struggling with four children, she moved to Arkansas for a job and a future, then moved to California for yet another job. Prayerfully, prayerfully, prayerfully she goes, always connecting with God's people for help and for prayer. Her husband is back with her now, and difficulties much larger than either of them made for themselves still hang over their lives and their children. But blessed? Is Karen blessed of God? Praying to be obedient and wise in difficult circumstances?

Yes, she would say so.

Joanna, a woman in our prayer group who has experienced many devastating and tragic reversals, has deepened and deepened in faith as she has faced years of sorrows and anxieties. One evening when she was walking home from her job at Wheaton College, tears began to flow. She had just faced another of life's disappointments, and the rest of the difficulties of recent months flooded back on her. She felt totally inadequate. As she walked in the cold air toward the sunset, she had no reason to hurry home, for no one was there. Endless questions arose within her. What was God doing?

That night, her last prayer was that God would give her some tangible evidence that he was using her to be a blessing to someone. She had prayed often before that he would use her to help someone, but now she also prayed, "Lord, if you are at work in my life, please show me. Give me some sign that my life is counting for *something.*"

In the next morning's mail Joanna received a card containing a cashier's check for fifty dollars and these words: "Your life and testimony are an encouragement to me. I wish this little gift could be multiplied over and over because of our Savior's love." It was signed simply, "A friend."

Joanna still does not know who sent the card, but its message and timing lifted her heart in humble gratitude. At the same time, she hesitates to tell of this incident, for she doesn't want others to be discouraged when their prayers do not bring tangible answers. Many, many of her own prayers for those she loves so much have seemed to have no effect.

Yet to speak to Joanna about prayer is to share with a woman who has seen God at work when many others have seen nothing at all. Like Solzhenitsyn, she sees God in deepest adversity, and she knows she truly is blessed. Joanna says, "Let God be God," with that contagious sparkle in her eyes that says God is indeed at work.

~

I can't resist being out here in the snow. I tromp a trail a deer broke for me in long leaps. Four prints . . . space . . . four prints . . . space. . . . Above, a jet's white trail cuts across the blue, drifting and diffusing crazily in the wind. I watch my feet again, then look up.

What's that? In the few seconds I looked down, the jet's vapor trail has become a series of flashes right into the heart of the sun, which is spraying out wide rays from behind a dark cloud. The jet's vapor has become a golden arrow, shot into the center. I half expect the whole thing to explode.

I watch my feet again, checking the deer trail. When I look up, it's all gone—vapor trail, golden arrow, dramatic brightness against the dark. The sun's rays now sneak timidly around the outer edges of the clouds.

In a clearing on a hilltop, snow on tall pines makes the branches sag in odd-shaped clumps. I stare and wonder at tree after tree, green against white, framed against the bright blue sky. At the field's edge are cedars and birch, thick with snow and draped over one another, sad but lovely.

The sky is getting dramatic again, dark clouds against

the bright rays that penetrate the woods, sparking the tops of trees with ice tricks. I marvel at the thought that this particular panorama can be seen only in this one spot in all the universe, at this moment, from this precise perspective.

I walk deep into the forest. Around me are thousands of saplings and hundreds of oak, wild cherry, dogwood, maple, birch, aspen, hickory, poplar. The wet snow on their trunks looks like snowball splatters, as if thousands of elves had thrown thousands of snowballs, and made thousands of hits. I smile at the thought, turning slowly round and round to take it all in, wondering how many splats there must be just within my sight. How many in all the Poconos? It would take millions of elves throwing millions of snowballs to decorate the Poconos.

All this from the hand of God.

Only occasionally do we spin in ecstasy surveying such wonders. More often we find ourselves on streets where the beautiful white is quickly plowed into curbs, where salt and cinders churn the snow into a gray-brown mush. The salt is splattered on our cars as we speed by, and the world takes on a dingy cast.

With all the salt and cinders in our lives, it's hard sometimes to see the hand of God at work. The gray dinginess of difficult times matches our inner failures. Are we blessed of God? Our prayers are for pure, white snow but all we see is gray mush.

"Blessed are you" say the angels and the Scriptures to those who seek and pray. "Call unto me, and I will show you great and mighty things."

But then come things like divorce and crucifixion and the day-by-day numbing of the spirit. Can we believe, in those times, that God is saying "Blessed are you"? When our prayers make us feel no closer to God? When what happens to us seems to say he is displeased with us?

Richie has called out to God and believed. He has prayed and studied the Scriptures. In prison he has run the marathon, been a chaplain's assistant, won all sorts of awards as president of the Jaycees. He corresponded with several Christians and then became engaged to one of them, an attractive young woman deeply committed to Christ. Surely it seemed God was answering his prayers. His fiancée visited us here on this mountain, and she and Richie looked forward to the day he would get out of prison and they could start their new life together. Year after year they prayed, and they saw what they believed were signs from God that Richie would be released. But year after year, Richie remained in prison. Not long ago, his fiancée broke the engagement.

Blessed are you, Richie. In the gray tedium of your cell and the prison grounds, blessed are you.

But it is very hard to see that blessedness.

So then we need to listen for another promise: Nothing can separate us from the love of Christ. Nothing.

At the end of Romans 8 we read that Christ is at the right hand of God making intercession for us so that nothing can separate us from his love. The apostle Paul says he is persuaded that neither life nor death nor angels nor powers—nothing that exists—can separate us from Christ's love. Not even the dingy feelings within, the sense that we cause our own troubles.

Nothing can separate us from our blessedness in him.

Johnny Copenhaver had been my close buddy since third grade in our little Smithfield School. One September, at the start of eighth grade, Johnny came back from a summer of hard work; he was no longer boyish like the rest of us, but thick-muscled and powerful. A group of us always played horses and riders, butting into each other, yanking and shoving, but now Johnny would never go down. No one shoved him too hard anymore, gentle Johnny.

He moved away for a time but came back our senior year of high school carrying a huge Bible with a leather-tooled cover. Brown-haired, good-looking, his muscles rippling snakes in his arms. Every day he got on the bus with a broad grin and that big Bible. He did crazy things, too, like letting not just a few, but every one of the girls on the bus before him. And he told everyone why he carried his Bible and did it with infectious good cheer, touching us like a Fisherman Peter come to life.

A year or two after high school, we were at Johnny's house polishing our shoes in preparation for his wedding. As his best man, I vowed as he put on his tux that I'd protect him from pranksters.

Johnny and his wife soon had a baby, and before the second one came I remember driving with him on a country road as he told me he was already a thousand dollars in debt. He went to New Jersey to get a better job, but he still struggled. He and his wife weren't getting along. I'd see Johnny in church once in awhile, but we only shook hands and talked about his job and babies. His exuberance was gone.

The last time I was with him was a cold winter day. He was separated from his wife; we sat in his old car, parked in a coal yard. I couldn't see his face or his eyes, but I knew the old Johnny had been slowly strangled somehow. "Come with me to Chicago," I offered. But he didn't come.

My mother told how she watched him in church, sitting with his little daughters beside him, smiling, singing hymns. A few days later he was sleeping alone in a cabin, and a gas leak killed him.

I sometimes wonder about all those prayers Johnny and I shared. His joy in serving God and his hearty personality were both shunted off halfway through the adventure. But those prayers still live. I still see Johnny's shining face announcing God's joy in the halls of our high school; I still see our group of boys in a classroom praying at noon for our school.

Blessed are you, Johnny.

Nothing can separate us from the love of Christ, for Jesus himself is at God's right hand interceding for us. Nothing—not our own failures, nor circumstances which defeat us—nothing can separate us from him. Not even death.

Before Elsbeth died, she and my cousin David had prayed earnestly for her healing. They experienced many remarkable answers to those prayers, including a lengthy remission when, according to the doctors, she was moments from death.

That temporary return to health enabled her to participate in a wedding, and she afterward told us of this experience.

As she walked down the aisle as matron of honor, she had to pace herself very carefully; she had not worn regular shoes for six months. Her eyesight was no longer good, and she had to squint to see the candles burning brightly in the distance. The soft light diffused into sparkling beads, like an other-worldly dawn, and it gave her a weird sensation. She knew David and her children were out there somewhere in the congregation watching as she walked painfully alone. *Will it be this way at my funeral,*—she wondered, *with me walking forward alone to meet Jesus?*

As she slowly made her way down the aisle, the candlelight beckoned her closer. She tightened her eyes. She loved the pink hues splattered with rays of reds and purples. *Here in this wedding are life, hope, and joy,* she thought. *It comes to us in such strange packages. But God does not play cat-and-mouse with us. In so many, many ways I know he loves me. And he loves David. Through it all, we trust him.*

She peered once more at the flickering candlelight, and as she slowly squeezed her eyes one more time, she watched it spray like colored surf into a thousand particles of dancing color. She thought, *Light is ahead. Life is ahead.*

Blessed are you, Elsbeth. Nothing can separate you from the love of Christ.

Despite evil and death, Gabriel's message sounds the good news. Paul's convictions ring clear. Oh, to celebrate what God does in the world! Oh, to have eyes that can see and ears that can hear the messages of angels.

10
LIVING BY HELPLESSNESS

I hike along the top of Kittatinny Mountain on the Appalachian Trail and come upon big birches trapped by frozen ice. They are like tall, willowy men bent double. I yank hard at one and it breaks free, but slabs of ice as big as a man's boots hang on. I kick at them and one falls off. I kick again, and finally the tree starts to rise.

Most of the other birches that were weighted to the ground by snow have risen halfway. It seems miraculous they could rise this far after half their skinny trunks were pinned against the ground, helpless until the sun began to rescue them.

But not all are rescued. Down the road, I see one has snapped—like a dead soldier broken over a fence.

Coming back near the house, I hear a deer snort an

oddly soft, diffident danger signal, almost like a sneeze. The deer rustles through thickets, then bounds into the open field, takes three leaps, and stops, turning her head to stare at me. After a full minute, two more run into the open. Then the three leap off in those high, archetype flights through the air.

I push through tangles of brush and sumac next to our little cinderblock barn where I once milked goats morning and night. Not much is left. The fence is flat and rusted, the barn collapsed. Sticking out from under green shingles are a few old, hand-hewn oak timbers from the original barn.

The graceful leaps of the deer remind me of the morning I found a small deer inside the eight-foot-high fence that surrounded the barnyard. I had no idea how it had gotten inside. As soon as the deer saw me, it ran as fast as it could toward the fence, gathering speed, but it couldn't clear the fence. Instead, the little deer smashed against the top and fell back, hard. It shook itself, stepped back and started running again, giving the attempt every ounce of energy possible. Once again the poor creature smashed against the top and fell hard to the ground.

The only other exit was through the barn. I left the door open and tried to herd the little deer through, but it cowered back, then ran off. From twenty yards away it started running again, in obvious desperation, determined to clear that fence. It leaped high, and its little body smashed so hard it bowed the whole fence, which just as quickly snapped back, throwing the animal down so brutally I thought its neck had broken.

Despite that, the deer's terror got him up, moved him back into position, and launched him against that fence again—and again and again—until finally he lay exhausted, mouth open, tongue out, eyes darting in panic.

I approached him now, touched him, spoke gently, patted his head. He lay still. My fingers felt little nubs of horns; he was a button buck. I lifted him, wanting to allay his terror but knowing I couldn't until I had walked him through the barn and set him safely outside the fence.

As I released him, he hesitated only a moment, and then bounded away.

And I wondered, as I watched him go, if the little buck ever understood that without my lifting him in my arms, he would have remained trapped, helpless.

Like us.

We Americans carry our pioneer self-reliance even into our spiritual lives. No fence is too high to leap. Like the button buck, we believe that with enough effort and energy we can scale whatever height might block us. If we smash against a fence, we try harder, refusing to believe we can't scale it. Only when events like rejection and illness and death and divorce finally crush us do we lie there, exhausted.

If we were to look up at those moments, we might see the God who stands by, waiting to lift us into his arms. We might allow his hands to lift us before we become bruised and broken on the fences. We might understand we really are helpless . . . like that young button buck . . . like those birch trees, locked into the ice, waiting for the sun.

Helpless? What are we talking about here? If people consider themselves helpless, how can they possibly face life?

Hallesby says it flat out: "Prayer is for the helpless." What does he mean by that? He insists on an idea that seems totally contradictory: that the power of prayer is, of all things, helplessness! How can this be? "I never grow weary of emphasizing our helplessness," Hallesby says, "for it is the decisive factor not only in our prayer life but in our whole relationship to God."

Each of us eventually becomes like the deer against the fence. Then, Hallesby says, that's the chance for a miracle. Where does he get such an idea? The truth is, Scripture is full of this paradox.

Paul said, "I will boast . . . about my weaknesses so that Christ's power may rest on me. That is why, for Christ's sake, I delight in weaknesses, in insults, in hardships, in persecutions, in difficulties, for when I am weak, then I am strong." And this, "But we have this treasure in jars of clay to show that this all surpassing power is from God and not from us."

But the evidence that has always struck me the strongest is Jesus' own statement: "Without the Father, I can do nothing."

He, Jesus Christ himself, Prince and King, could do nothing. He said so. And he spent all night in prayer, "helpless" before the Father. Only as he was vitally linked to the Father and obeyed him did the forces of evil collapse under the most helpless of acts, stretching out his arms to be crucified.

Everything in our culture strikes against this. I stood in church one morning as a college student said with a note of discouragement, "All the graduation addresses tell us, 'It's a tough world out there, and you've got to get tough.'" That is the world's theme song: "When the going gets tough, the tough get going."

But in reality the world is so subtly, brutally, fatally tough that we've got to get—*helpless.*

Helpless, simply because we are. We are no match for evil powers. If Jesus couldn't stand alone, it's clear that our actions apart from the Father are just so much leaping at fences.

That's one reality. But then Hallesby, who of all people makes so much of our helplessness, turns around and describes prayer as powerful. He refers to the time Jesus was about to ascend into heaven, leaving his uneducated eleven disciples with a superhuman task. He commanded those frightened men to go out and make Christ-worshipers of all nations.

Imagine! Eleven common laborers, terrified to their sandals by Jesus' executioners who had been known to crucify three thousand in a day's work—these men were supposed to make an impact on the entire world.

But then Hallesby says, almost like a science-fiction writer revealing a secret weapon, "He had equipped them with prayer." And he quotes Jesus' familiar but still astounding words, "Nothing shall be impossible to you."

Nothing shall be impossible to you! We all know the startling statements Jesus made about prayer moving mountains, and about two or more agreeing in prayer and anything at all happening in response. How do we who are helpless connect with that kind of power?

Some time ago, four of us conducted a *Leadership* journal interview with Henri Nouwen and Richard Foster on the subject of prayer and the spiritual life. We met in a conference room between the terminals at O'Hare Airport in Chicago. Although we knew Richard, none of us had met Henri Nouwen before, and we wondered what this Catholic priest and author would be like in person.

I was prepared for him to be warm and open; but I was shocked by the extent of his instant vulnerability. When he entered the room, the fiftyish Dutch scholar wearing horn-rimmed glasses grinned boyishly, and before a few moments were up he was sharing experiences with us that revealed his personal weaknesses. He spoke of recently being in the Pacific Northwest, exhausted spiritually and totally at the end of himself; the intervention of some Christian brothers who took him on a retreat pulled him up from despair. Never had I seen such immediate vulnerability. He was not simply being open with friends; he was stripping away all pretense of competence and strength in front of four Protestant journalists he had never met.

As our discussion about spiritual disciplines and God's work in us continued, each of us participating shared various insights. But what struck me most forcibly was

Nouwen's sense of total weakness contrasted with the power of his being a fragile vessel open to God's enabling.

After driving home, I walked for hours on the Glen Ellyn streets, filled with joy and a sense of power. But not in the least *my* power. I sensed in a fresh way that God runs his universe as he pleases, and that he will do battle with evil on his own terms and in his own way. If I wanted to be a part of that, I could open my hands and body and life. For me, only rarely do prayer and circumstance merge as they did that day, so that the hellishness of life seems irrelevant, the bitter mysteries God's problem. Nouwen's stance of helplessness, his spirit of weakness, put "all things" into God's hands and opened the way to praise and gratitude.

Such helplessness doesn't ignore skills and strengths. As a Harvard and Princeton professor, Henri Nouwen had used his gifts. But if we want to live by God's surprises and see him at work, we start with the recognition that we really are "little fellows in the world after all," and that our powers and skills become significant only when they are empowered in a far deeper way than we can see.

At moments, our helplessness becomes as apparent as our inability to leap to the moon. I sensed that when my cousin Lois died, when Johnny's marriage broke up, when Elsbeth lay dying of leukemia, when Richie was being tried for Mrs. Prosser's murder. We sense it every week in our prayer group as we share our heartaches, our deep personal failures, the tragic events in our families.

Catherine Marshall saw this as she was writing her first book, *A Man Called Peter.* When she cried out to God, "I'm whipped, helpless," the response that came was, "Helpless? Your problem is helplessness?" She remembered, then, Jesus' words that apart from him, the vine, we can do nothing. "Was helplessness, then, not such an unusual state?" she asked. "Could it be we human beings actually are helpless, but most of the time don't know it? Could the realization of it be the first step out? Could our inadequacy become our greatest asset when it becomes the open door to God's adequacy?"

Then Catherine Marshall remembered that "the clearest response I'd ever gotten from God came out of the most abject helplessness of my life," a time when she had had tuberculosis. A few days after gaining these insights, a "courageous experimenter with prayer" visited her. She prayed for Catherine—to her astonishment—at exactly her points of helplessness about writing her book. "Coincidence?" Catherine Marshall asks. "I don't think so. I felt the Spirit of God had directed the prayer."

A year ago, Jeanette and I brought our first foster child into our home. Billy, two-and-a-half, had just gotten his leg out of a cast. Some thought his father had broken it. Bright, always ready for a hug, Billy won our hearts instantly.

One afternoon I found him sitting quietly, staring into a corner, his expression sad, his mind and emotions obviously elsewhere. I wondered what he was thinking about. Then he looked up at me and pleaded, "See Daddy, please! Please!" He paused, then he stretched out the word, imploring me: "See, Daddy. Please!"

He wanted his daddy, whatever his daddy might have done to him. I hugged him, and all I could say was, "Soon, Billy."

I was truly helpless.

Take in foster children, and you realize quickly how helpless any of us are to "solve the problems" of these children's lives. It is an arena for prayer, but also a metaphor for the complexity of spiritual warfare and our helplessness to crash the fences or melt the ice alone.

Hezekiah knew this. When enemy armies besieged his fortified city, telling his people in salty language just what they would do to them, Hezekiah laid it all out before the Lord. Hezekiah knew how to be helpless before God, and he knew how to pray. And God delivered him.

On the other hand, Jacob had never learned this lesson. He had lied and schemed his way through life until he was up against the fence. He was afraid his brother, whom he had wronged, would finally kill him. He wrestled with God all through the night until finally his hip ligament was loosened. Only then, when he became helpless before God, did Jacob become a different person—so different that God changed his name to Israel.

None of us can conquer the enemy armies that suddenly appear all around us. None of us can change our self-centered selves. But when we acknowledge that, when we are helpless before God in prayer, that very helplessness enables remarkable things to happen.

A new day. Snow again, deep and heavy. Midmorning, I tramp through it to the road and see a hunter in bright orange from cap to boots coming toward me. "Terrible getting through that swamp," he says.

"See anything?"

"Got a shot at some turkeys on top of the mountain, but the snow is so thick, my birdshot didn't do anything."

I take the back-ridge trail down to the Gap, making reasonable time through the thick, heavy snow. But coming back by the creek, trees and bushes drape the narrow paths. Today, the birches remind me of tall women pulled down by their hair and frozen into the snow, spines bent. I break them loose, shake great clumps of snow away; they rise a foot off the ground and hang limp. The laurel has become impenetrable wedges blocking the path. I crash through the labyrinth, making slow progress. The way has become nearly impassable. I try getting off the trail, but laurel extends in every direction.

It's tough going. Snow is down my neck; I'm sweating. I decide to switch to the road, but puddles its full width make it worse than the trail; under a thin film of ice, the water is deep. I cannot pass on the edges because saplings and big bushes are bent over the road, giant, soggy blankets of white pressing them down. I try to jump and twist and negotiate, but cannot move forward without getting my feet soaked.

I climb the steep hill beside the road. A hundred yards up is a fresh deer trail; I follow it but make slow progress in the deep snow, careful to keep the mountain in view to make sure I'm heading home. I am awed at the amount of snow everywhere. How helpless is man against nature! After an hour of hard slogging, I make it home and wearily undress and shower.

It gets dark early in November. After reading and writing a while, I turn on the television. *High Plains Drifter,* a Clint Eastwood movie, comes on. It begins with the scruffy but steely Clint riding a nondescript nag into town, staring down assorted Western stereotypes. Three gunmen in the saloon tell him that some people consider the pace in this town too fast. Clint walks off with his beer; they follow him to the barber shop and start to rough him up. Under the barber's sheet, Clint holds a pistol. They keep roughing him up until he efficiently blows all three into eternity.

We learn, as the story goes on, that the entire town is guilty. Some are guilty of brutally murdering a man with a bullwhip. Others watched it happen and didn't lift a finger to stop it. The whole place is rotten, cowardly, greedy, wanton.

The high plains drifter eventually gets control of the town and has the whole place painted red; then he personally paints over the original sign at the edge of town with the word "Hell."

Hell Town.

In the final violent scenes the drifter proceeds to purge the town. With a bullwhip, he executes the three who murdered, by the same method, the man he is avenging. The town becomes an inferno of death and destruction to match its name.

It's a creative, well-crafted script, but I always feel ambivalent about Clint Eastwood movies. A few nights ago they brought back his Dirty Harry role in a made-for-television episode. Mimicking the original movie, he said with loathing to the despicable man brutalizing a woman, "Make my day!" and then blasted him into a long fall and a dramatic crash through multi-colored windows. It's a strange feeling—this urge to identify with Eastwood while at the same time sensing the over-simplifications.

Such revenge films have wide appeal. I'm told one survey indicates a majority of young people picked out Clint Eastwood as the person they most want to emulate. What does this say of us?

It's natural to share Dirty Harry's rage at blatant evil. We know that when good men do nothing, evil wins. Yes, we are drawn to a man who will stand up to overpowering evil—like Bonhoeffer attempting to kill Hitler, despite all the might of the Nazis. We respect the granite resolve of the high plains drifter as he speaks with unflinching honesty, a man who swallows whatever timidity whispers in his soul and stands against evil.

What, then, disturbs me as I watch? What in me resists being carried along in the final paroxysm of violence?

Violence and revenge. Sweet, sweet revenge! How the audience waits for those moments when evil is blasted away with a stunned look of disbelief on its face—not a man's face, but an actor portraying a beastly subhuman beneath contempt.

In real life, however, revenge does not appease the rage and grief of our hearts.

In contrast, we read of Corrie Ten Boom's forgiveness of her Nazi jailer; we read of a murdered bus driver's widow who forgave her husband's killer; we read of a mother writing to forgive the man in prison convicted of murdering her daughter. From Belfast to New York City to Beirut we read of those who in obedience to Christ forgive even the worst and most beastly of men and women and thereby find peace. "Vengeance is mine, saith the Lord."

Who are these creatures of total evil we enjoy seeing killed on the screen? Figments of fiction. Demons may be pure evil, but not human beings made in God's image.

We are called to envision even the worst human being as perfect in Christ Jesus. Is the gospel powerful enough for that? Is Christ powerful enough? Yes, surely he is, for we have also read of mobsters, rapists, child abusers, and murderers coming into vital relationships with their Maker. We even read of the proud and self-righteous receiving him. The truth is, if we put ourselves above even one other human being, we have not yet seen the depths of rebellion in our own hearts.

Perhaps the most famous cartoon caption of all time is Pogo's. He and his cohorts have been tracking "the enemy" through the woods when they suddenly find they have been following their own footprints. Pogo then declares, "We have found the enemy, and he is us!"

Wesley said, "There, but for the grace of God, go I." It is hard to think about that watching *Magnum Force.* It is hard to admit we share a heritage of sin with every other human being. Although society must root out evil behavior, as individuals we are totally dependent upon God for any internal "goodness."

On the other hand, each of us is made in God's image—even Hitler, our twentieth-century archetype of evil. C. S. Lewis quotes a pastor who had met Hitler.

"What was he like?" Lewis asked.

"Like any man. Like Christ," the pastor replied. He was, presumably, speaking of God's image even in the worst of men.

Another Christian was asked during the Nazi reign of terror what he would do if he met Hitler. He said, "I would pray for him."

Only God could change Hitler. Or the men and women of Hell Town. Or us. For, like the high plains drifter, we may go into Hell Town seeking revenge, but seeking justice requires the light and the power of God. Without God, we are helpless. Not helpless to take up arms and fight evil; that we can do. But helpless to transcend our own sinfulness and arrogance.

Only God can turn our helplessness into prayer for the Hitlers of the world, and for our neighbors, and for ourselves, that grace may be far greater than our sin.

Imagine the town of Jerusalem with its corrupt officials, hypocritical Pharisees, destroyers of widows, despoilers of God's honor. Here is a town with the smoke of hell in its nostrils, a town ready-made for the high plains drifter. He rides into town on a nondescript nag, unwashed from long travel, intent on his mission.

Beside him, riding on a donkey, peering at the city, we see a man equally resolute, equally good at telling it straight to the city's despoilers. And through the mind of the man on the donkey run these thoughts about the city's leaders: "Ye are of your father, the devil . . . Oh, Jerusalem, Jerusalem, how often would I have gathered you under my arms like a hen gathers its chicks. But ye would not . . . Without the Father, I can do nothing."

The high plains drifter rides beside him thinking of those same men with blood on their hands and evil in their hearts. Quietly, with steel in his soul, he is planning, planning, planning, savoring the rage within. He rides into the once-glorious but now hellish Jerusalem, ready to even the score.

And what would happen to the high plains drifter in real life—in real life, mind you? He would make his attempt and be blasted away by the powerful forces of evil. He would be laid to rest without his revenge, "for those who live by the sword shall die by the sword."

In real life, the equally determined Jesus rode his little donkey into the Hell Town he loved. He who could call down legions of angels and all the power of creation rode into Jerusalem defenseless. He prayed to his Father that the terrible events ahead might pass from him, but he did not flinch. He did not tell his accusers, "Make my day!" and then blast them into eternity. He loved the worst of them—the proud religious leaders—and he was hung up naked and was crucified.

Helpless.

But from his obedience to the Father, his helplessness, came resurrection power to conquer death and evil forever. "Without the Father," said Jesus, "I can do nothing."

If we could see the forces of good and evil encircling us—if we could see God versus Satan as Jesus did—we would understand. We are like aborigines with bows and arrows standing between nuclear armies.

Thielicke understood that. During the worst time of persecution from the Nazis, he stood up for Christ, and then he was able to say joyfully, almost exultantly, "I'm through. I've made it. Now what comes of it is God's responsibility. Now I have summoned God into the fray. Is it not more than sufficient . . . to eliminate one's self, to taste the blessedness of knowing that God himself rises up to perform his mighty works, and that in the midst of the earth where the powers clash and the terrible battle rages, I have been transferred into the unspeakable peace and safety of Heaven, which is now breaking through and unfurling the banner of the kingdom?"

Thielicke also said, "I call into the arena him by whom I live. It is with him you have to deal, and not with me."

We call God into the arena. In our helplessness, we pray, and the power of heaven is ours.

Midnight. I hear sounds on the roof. Perhaps the red squirrels my dad thought he had gotten rid of? Something swishes and falls heavily. I turn on the outside lights. The snow is melting, coming down in sheets off the roof. The thaw has come.

Yesterday, the trees were helplessly bowed down by snow. Cedars, spruce, aspen, all caught and bent—even the birch I had shaken loose hung disconsolately a foot off the ground. But the thaw will change everything.

Tomorrow the sun will shine again. And like God's work through prayer, it will release the captives, break the impasses, and bring warmth to the world's creatures.

11
LIVING BY HOPE

All these weeks walking the woods I've wondered about the albino. Once, near the red berries where we had seen it, a deer crossed the road and I heard another in the woods. But no albino.

Now I am walking Dolack's old driveway, and I see something white. I keep my eyes on it, moving slowly to right and left so trees won't block the view. As I get closer, I see it's large and very white. Too white. Finally I recognize it—an abandoned washing machine.

I turn onto a wide trail through the woods. Instantly I realize something odd is on the ground to my left. It records in my brain as a goat, like one of the white Saanens I used to milk. But the next second I realize it's the albino, a full-grown doe. She is lying placidly on a grassy knoll, soaking up the sun. Two smaller deer are with her. On seeing me, she stands up and slowly walks away. There she is, small black spots on her shoulder but otherwise perfectly white, trailing off into the woods with the others.

I follow them, trying to keep her in sight. The albino is far down the mountain; if she weren't white, I couldn't see her at this distance. She makes a sharp switchback. I reverse direction also and head straight for the road I know they'll have to cross. When I get there, I see her already into the woods on the other side, a moving white shape soon gone.

White deer have always captured the imagination. Do people who aren't looking get to see such ghostly shapes in the woods? Not often. The man in the truck had been looking for her as he drove, and that's why he saw her. That time, I had not been thinking albino at all, and had missed her.

One can go through the woods, or through life, and miss elusive surprises—sunsets, deer, Christmas trees, and strange stirrings in our lives. God's surprises, like the albino, are out there in our own life stories, but usually their meaning slips away into the forest, unseen.

Some people seek that meaning with tenacious intensity. Daniel was like that. Prayer was so at the core of his life that his enemies could only attack him by getting his prayers declared illegal. He didn't flinch; he continued to commune with God three times a day, and though thrown into the lion's den, God kept him completely safe.

The well-known story is a remarkable example of the power of prayer. But other incidents in Daniel's life show prayer's mysterious connection with beings from other worlds. For instance, Daniel says, "I was praying and confessing my sin and the sins of my people and desperately pleading with the Lord my God for Jerusalem"—and in the middle of this earnest prayer—"Gabriel, whom I had seen in the earlier vision, flew swiftly to me." Here is this same Gabriel, who hundreds of years later would announce Jesus' birth to Mary and John's to Zechariah.

Then Daniel describes one of the most mysterious events in Scripture. For three full weeks he had been praying and fasting. "One day in early April, as I was standing beside the great Tigris River, I looked up and suddenly there before me stood a person robed in linen garments, with a belt of purest gold around his waist, and glowing, lustrous skin! From his face came blinding flashes like lightning, and his eyes were pools of fire; his arms and feet shone like polished brass, and his voice was like the roaring of a great multitude of people."

A rather dramatic answer to prayer! The men with him saw nothing, but "they were suddenly filled with unreasoning terror and ran to hide." Daniel, himself terrified, fell flat on his face, too weak to move.

"But a hand touched me and lifted me," Daniel says, "And I heard his voice—'O Daniel, greatly beloved of God.'" The man with the voice like a roaring multitude tells him not to be afraid! Then this person from another world goes on to relate an intriguing incident. He explains that as soon as Daniel had started praying three weeks before, he had been sent to meet him. "But for twenty-one days the mighty evil spirit who overrules the kingdom of Persia blocked my way. Then Michael, one of the top officers of the heavenly army, came to help me, so that I was able to break through these spirit rulers of Persia."

What is that all about? We pray, and orders go forth, but angels must battle through evil forces to get to us? Are some of these mysterious conflicts the reason we must intercede for others, and for our nation, and for the world? What really is going on as we kneel to pray?

Still weak from terror, Daniel says, "How can such a

person as I even talk to you? For my strength is gone and I can hardly breathe."

The other-worldly being with glowing, lustrous skin and eyes like pools of fire says, "God loves you very much; don't be afraid! Calm yourself; be strong. Yes, strong!"

Then the heavenly messenger says that after he tells Daniel the message, he will have a major battle ahead. "I will go again to fight my way back, past the prince of Persia; and after him, the prince of Greece. Only Michael, the angel who guards your people Israel, will be there to help me."

Few people have centered their lives in prayer as intensely as Daniel. Perhaps that's why we see in his life something of what may really be going on when we pray: God's forces and evil powers at war, yet the assurance that we are greatly loved of God and that we should not be afraid. In prayer, we can call on forces far beyond our imagination.

I stand on a ledge called Eagle's Cliff which juts out high above the country club and golf course. For miles in the distance mountains rise languorously from the morning mists, reminding me of Scotland or Ireland. From far below, a ruckus startles me. Something big and noisy is crashing through the forest, snapping and cracking dead limbs and brush. A hunter? Peering down, I spy three deer, spooked by something, running with uncharacteristic noise.

A gravel road leads into the woods; a few steps into it and I see an odd-shaped building. As I get closer I realize it's an abandoned ski lift, with a tree grown up through its cable wheel. The tree, thick as my thigh, has long been dead. Decades ago, people had wanted to make this a major ski resort; then the government took over the land.

I walk the surrounding woods, past flat-stone fireplaces without chimneys, standing like hunched old men in the woods, the only remnants of bulldozed homes. A wall ahead of me turns out to be a stone well about three feet high and ten feet wide. This was a serious well, made of fieldstones and mortar. The round stones, about fist size, are precisely placed; I can imagine the builder showing his wife each day's careful progress. I peer inside. At ground level is a Miller Beer can!

Today's trash desecrates yesterday's treasure. A tree grows through someone's dream. The stoneworks of craftsmen stand eerily alone in the forest.

Fragments of former lives.

The ridge to the waterfall is soggy from the melting snow. As I get closer, I realize how much more forceful and deep the creek is. Between the evergreens, white water rushes down the chute and then to the rectangular pool above the falls. Days ago, the creek was half this deep; in summer, it will be a trickle.

Like the flow of God's purpose in our lives, the stream is both predictable and unpredictable, full of surprises yet also constant. The trees and trails remain the same; the water changes in season. Like the pilgrim in *Pilgrim's Progress,* the traveler following these waters finds everything new, yet—like God's holiness and his compassion for us—always the same. The hiker finds both dull trickles and lively currents, impassable gulleys and open expanses, dangerous gorges and safe fields.

The wide, flat wet stone, green and slick, is certainly not one of the safe places. Just above the falls, this stretch of descending rock with the water coursing beside it is the only way down. "Very, very careful now," I am thinking, "there's nothing to hold on to. Move slowly . . . move slowly." And sure enough, though I am hardly moving, I fall, splat! on my back and elbow. I wince and rub away the sharp pain.

The water in the pool is much more forceful than before, curving out in frothy, self-assured power and excitement toward the falls, rushing, rushing like thousands of white birds. Where I crossed over last time is a turgid current. If I tried it now, I'd cascade down the chute, into the battered sticks floating at the edge, then over the falls. This is not a time for foolhardiness.

I step under some trees, watching the exhilarating white power. "I wish it were always like this," I think, but just as quickly remind myself that "to every time, there is a season." There are moments in a believer's life when the pulse is quickened and the linkage through prayer seems like a mighty force, like those hours of walking after the Henri Nouwen interview or those answers to prayer on the bus trip to Kansas City. But it's unrealistic to expect white-water exhilaration at every bend in the forest.

To get to the base of the falls, I have to climb to the trail far above it. The air is misty as I start to descend. I grab at branches as I go, slipping in the wet, thick pine needles, stabbing with my feet at roots to keep my balance. The waterfall is far larger than when I was here before. Its pace has quickened. It seems proud of its energetic, all-white, pulsing self, spraying droplets on me forty feet away. The air from it strikes and chills.

A primeval world rises around me, sheer rocks with ferns and moss on either side; above that, conifers rise hundreds of feet into the air, surrounded by laurel, dramatic in the mist. At the lip of the falls a thick, ancient pine squats massively on a flat slab of rock. A strong wind, it seems, would send it all crashing over the falls.

Somehow, despite the mature trees, the glade seems

a young world, with the water the living creature, the plunger, the acrobat, the royal performer. A squirrel climbing in a high tree is a mere bit player. I spin full circle. The mist closes in from all directions, closing me into a moment when God's mighty hand of creation seems fresh as Eden.

"Sing praises to God." Yes. Despite dangers and sorrows, we rejoice. "Enter into his gates with thanksgiving," says the psalmist, "and into his courts with praise." Praise for who God is. Praise for his great love at Christmas and his great sacrifice at Easter. Praise for the way he works in people: for Karen and Richie who don't give up; for parents who love me and foster kids and anyone in need; for all who take in the children of the world; for colleagues praying through temptations and opportunities. Praise him for his work in each of us.

Praise. Thanksgiving. Gratitude. According to hospital studies, gratitude is the most healthful emotion a patient can experience. We are *made* for gratitude and thanksgiving.

Praise for this moment. Praise for his mighty works in our lives. Praise for what's ahead, for the best is yet to come.

A Christian who was dying said to a friend of mine, "You know, I've had a good life, but not an overly exciting one. I didn't get to explore new worlds like Columbus or go on some great expedition. But my chance lies ahead. My challenge is the next life. I'm excited about what's coming!"

What *does* lie ahead? For those who believe—for those who are like little children—the wonders are hinted at all through the Scriptures. In our new bodies, what new colors will we see? What sounds and music will we hear? What planets will we explore? With what unknown creatures of God will we converse? What adventures lie before us who are loved by the God who created this waterfall rising before me, and the great Niagaras of earth, and all the adventures and stories and creativity that ever will be?

Praise him for what is to come. Praise him for that moment in the next world when we say, as E. Rooney expressed it: "How could I ever have dreamed so sweet a morning after so dark a night?"

Despite all our fears of what's ahead, praise him for his assurance that as Christ rose from the dead, so will we. As Christ was welcomed in the heavenly places, so will we be.

Years ago I would often write late at night in a Big Boy restaurant, and the background music played there was a tape of popular songs, including "Tie a Yellow Ribbon." I heard it dozens of times, and when I'd pause to listen, would always be touched.

The song tells of a man who has been sent to prison. He has served his time and is now coming home on the bus. But he admits that she who once loved him has every right to reject him. He's to blame. So he has written to tell her that if she forgives him, she should "tie a yellow ribbon 'round the old oak tree." If there's no yellow ribbon, he'll just go riding by on the bus. As the miles roll by all the man thinks about is that oak tree. When he gets home, will there be a yellow ribbon on it?

The song ends in triumph with the entire busload of people cheering as the man sees not one but a *hundred* yellow ribbons on that old oak tree! His lover not only forgives him but exuberantly welcomes him home.

Like the man on the bus, we are fearful of death and what's ahead. We know our own hearts, and we wonder if God will really forgive us, let alone celebrate our coming.

But Scripture assures us of God's welcome: "If we confess our sins, he is faithful and just to forgive us our sins, and to cleanse us from all unrighteousness." The yellow ribbons will be there. We will go as little children, full of wonder, to the party, to our reunion with him.

Nevertheless, we are apprehensive. In response to heavenly visions, Daniel, John, and Isaiah each fell down in terror. But they were touched, strengthened, and purified by the experience. Each was told not to be afraid; they were loved of God.

A letter sent to Catherine Marshall describes one man's experience the day his wife died: "I left the house at 1:00 P.M. . . . when I returned at 5:30, she was lying on the bathroom floor. There were no goodbyes. She was gone.

"It was probably between 1:00 and 2:00 A.M. before I got to bed and to sleep that night. However, at very early dawn I began to be conscious again of the world around me and of another world. Our bedroom is an enclosed sleeping porch at the rear of the house with windows on three sides.

"Margaret had loved the out-of-doors along with music and birds.

"How can I describe to you my experience of that dawn? All I can say is that Margaret was there and I was there at a little distance observing it all. As a navy officer during the war, I found myself thinking of the ceremony when an admiral is piped aboard. It was as if the boundaries between earth and heaven were obliterated and Margaret was being piped aboard. She was entering her heavenly home in a blaze of glory with the birds singing that morning as I have never heard them sing before or since. It was as if ten thousand angels were crying, 'Joy! Joy! Joy! Here comes Margaret! Everybody out! Everybody out! Here comes Margaret!'"

Yellow ribbons and shouts of angels. Is that how it will be? The New Testament is full of such hope.

I remember standing in the basement of the church with David the day of Elsbeth's funeral. We said to each other, "It seems so strange, now that she is gone, that we aren't still praying for her." And we said to God right then and there, "Bless Elsbeth! Whatever she is experiencing right now, give her great joy!"

Maybe at that very moment Elsbeth was experiencing something like the vision of Margaret's husband. I can just see Elsbeth, who told us how she slowly squeezed her eyes at the wedding and watched light spray into dancing color. I can envision her going forth with joy to her God and being piped into heaven with thousands of angels shouting: "Here comes Elsbeth! Joy! Joy! Joy! Everybody out to welcome her home! Here comes Elsbeth!"

And when Lois crashed into that culvert and David quoted at her funeral that a corn of wheat must die, was she even then being piped into new worlds with joy and exultation: "Here comes Lois! Rejoice! Here she comes!"

And my dearest friend Johnny who died so young. Did the heavenly hosts gather with a woodsy, foot-banging welcome for this man of the mountains? Did they make the hills shake with delighted cries of "Here comes Johnny!" With his big grin and his loving heart adding wonders to heaven, I can hear the celebration: "Here comes Johnny! Joy! Joy! Joy! Everybody out to welcome Johnny!"

The mist is in my face. It's too cold and wet to stay in the world of the falls. I climb to the ridge, grabbing laurel to pull myself up, careful of the slippery mush of the pine carpet. At the top, I pause and look down at the waterfall cascading wildly to the brink, then plunging far below, rushing over a jumble of dark rocks in a tangle of white water. But downstream the water flows quietly under a bridge, thick and fast and down-to-business.

We are not yet being welcomed to Paradise. The *ruach* is still to come into our lives. Storms and breeze, violence and calm, the Creator will bring his surprises out of all of them.

We do not yet see face to face like Elsbeth or Lois or Johnny; we see darkly, but hopefully, like Habakkuk. We live by God's surprises, and the ultimate surprises are ahead, beyond the grave, where our prayers will become communication face to face.

Habakkuk accepted enigmas and sorrows as part of his dealings with God, and he believed the promises. "You split the earth with rivers," Habakkuk wrote, "the mountains saw you and writhed. Torrents of water swept by; the deep roared."

I heard and my heart pounded,
my lips quivered at the sound;
decay crept into my bones,
and my legs trembled.
Yet I will wait patiently . . . .
I will be joyful in God my Savior.

NOTES

Especially helpful in exploring this volume's themes were the many books of collected sermons by Helmut Thielicke, the multi-volume devotional books by Oswald Chambers, the sermons and autobiographical writings of Frederick Buechner, and various works by Peter and Catherine Marshall. A few specific references and additional sources are included below.

3. Living by Surprise

Helmut Thielicke, *Our Heavenly Father* (Grand Rapids: Baker Book House, 1960).

Helmut Thielicke, *How to Believe Again* (Philadelphia: Fortress Press, 1972), 49.

Oswald Chambers, *So Send I You* (Christian Literature Crusade, 1930), 34, 35.

4. Living by Persistence

S. Rickly Christian, *Alive* (Grand Rapids: Zondervan/Campus Life, 1983), 104.

M. Scott Peck, *The Road Less Traveled* (New York: Simon and Schuster, 1980).

O. Hallesby, *Prayer* (Minneapolis: Augsburg, 1931), 153.

5. Living by Adventure

Catherine Marshall, *To Live Again* (New York: Fawcett, 1957), 33.

Virginia Stem Owens, "Prayer—Into the Lion's Jaws," *Christianity Today* (19 November 1976).

6. Living by Faith

Annie Dillard, *Pilgrim at Tinker Creek* (New York: Harper's Magazine Press, 1974).
Thielicke, *Believe Again,* 212.
Thielicke, *Heavenly Father.*

7. Living by Mystery

Bob Benson, *He Speaks Softly* (Waco: Word Books, 1985), 64, 65.

8. Living by Intercession

John V. Taylor, *The Go-Between God* (New York: Oxford University Press, 1972), 233.
E. G. Carré, *Praying Hyde* (South Plainfield, N.J.: Bridge Publishing Inc., 1982), 136–137.

10. Living by Helplessness

Hallesby, *Prayer,* 26, 60–63.
Marshall, *Live Again,* 125, 126.
Helmut Thielicke, *Life Can Begin Again* (Philadelphia: Fortress Press, 1963), 21.

11. Living by Hope

Marshall, *Live Again,* 168.